MW01258972

The
CHORUS
BOOK

CONTEMPORARY
and
TRADITIONAL
FAVORITES

Compiled by KEN BIBLE

LILLENAS
PUBLISHING COMPANY

lillenas.com

Awesome God

R. M.

RICH MULLINS

Our God is an awe-some God; He reigns from heav-en a-bove With wis - dom, pow'r and love. Our God is an awe - some God! Our God! Our God is an awe - some God!

2   All Hail King Jesus

Revelation 4:8

D. M.

DAVE MOODY

All hail King Je - sus,____ All hail Em - man - u - el,____

King of Kings, Lord of Lords, Bright Morn-ing Star.____

____ And thro' - out e - ter - ni - ty, I'll sing His prais - es,

____ And I'll reign with Him thro' - out e - ter - ni - ty.____

Glorify Thy Name

John 12:28

3

D. A.

DONNA ADKINS

1. Fa - ther, we love You, we wor - ship and a - dore You;
2. Je - sus, we love You, we wor - ship and a - dore You;
3. Spir - it, we love You, we wor - ship and a - dore You;

Glo - ri - fy Thy name in all the earth.

Glo - ri - fy Thy name, glo - ri - fy Thy name,

Glo - ri - fy Thy name in all the earth.

4

Isn't He?

J. W.

JOHN WIMBER

Is - n't He beau - ti - ful? Beau - ti - ful,
Is - n't He won - der - ful? Won - der - ful,

is - n't He? Prince of Peace,_____ Son of God,_____
is - n't He?

is - n't He?_____ Coun - sel - or,_____ Al -

might - y God,_____ is - n't He,_____ is - n't He, is - n't He?

Make Me a Servant

5

K. W.

KELLY WILLARD

6 Bless the Lord, O My Soul

Psalm 103:1

Adapted

Unknown

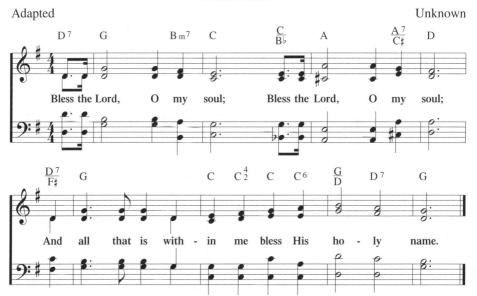

Bless the Lord, O my soul; Bless the Lord, O my soul;

And all that is with - in me bless His ho - ly name.

7 He Is Exalted

1 Chronicles 29:11

T. P.

TWILA PARIS

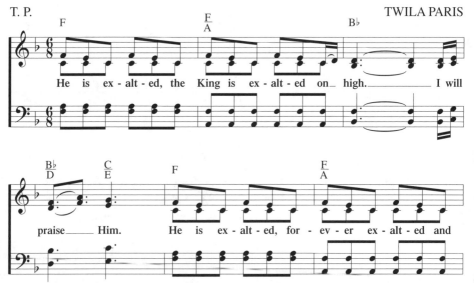

He is ex - alt - ed, the King is ex - alt - ed on_ high._____ I will

praise_____ Him. He is ex - alt - ed, for - ev - er ex - alt - ed and

8 His Name Is Wonderful

A. M.

AUDREY MIEIR

His name is Won-der-ful; His name is Won-der-ful; His name is

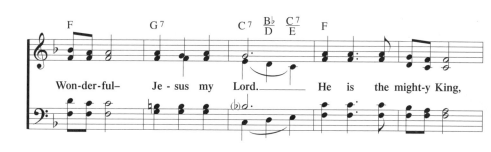

Won-der-ful– Je - sus my Lord._____ He is the might-y King,

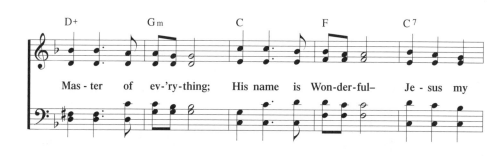

Mas - ter of ev-'ry-thing; His name is Won-der-ful– Je - sus my

Lord. He's the great Shep-herd, the Rock of all a - ges,

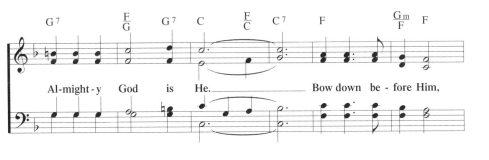

Al-might-y God is He.____ Bow down be - fore Him,

love and a - dore Him; His name is Won-der-ful— Je - sus, my Lord.

I Love Him

9

1 John 4:19

Traditional

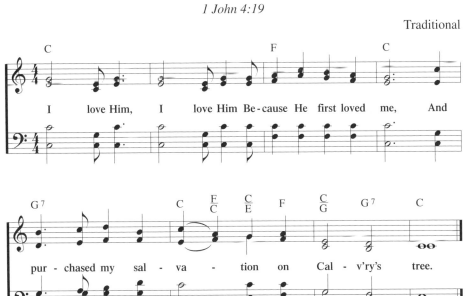

I love Him, I love Him Be - cause He first loved me, And

pur - chased my sal - va - - tion on Cal - v'ry's tree.

10

I Know the Lord Will Make a Way

Unknown

God Will Make a Way

D. M.

DON MOEN

12 Take My Life

S. U.

SCOTT UNDERWOOD

13 Let's Just Praise the Lord

W. J. G. and G. G.

WILLIAM J. and GLORIA GAITHER

More Precious than Silver

14

Proverbs 8:10-11

L. D.

LYNN DESHAZO

Lord, You are more pre-cious than sil-ver.

Lord, You are more cost-ly than gold.

Lord, You are more beau-ti-ful than dia-monds

and noth-ing I de-sire com-pares with You.

15 I Exalt Thee

Psalm 97:9

P. S., JR.   PETE SANCHEZ, JR.

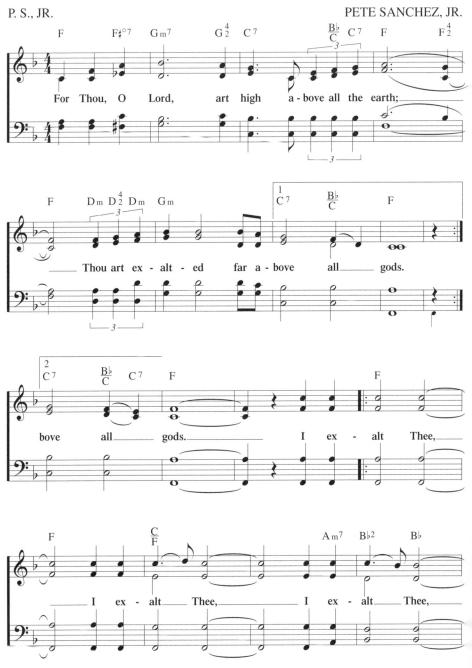

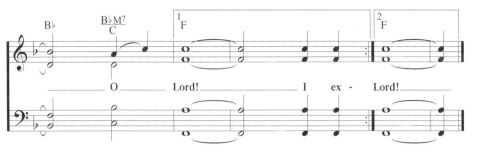

We Will Lift Up the
Name of the Lord

16

M. L.

MOSIE LISTER

17

He's Able

2 Corinthians 9:8

P. E. P.

PAUL E. PAINO
Arranged by Lyndell Leatherman

He's a - ble, He's a - ble, I know He's a - ble; I know my

Lord is a - ble to car-ry me through. through.

He healed the bro - ken - heart-ed and set the cap - tive free; He

made the lame to walk a - gain and caused the blind to see.

Every Day with Jesus

18

ROBERT C. LOVELESS

WENDELL P. LOVELESS

Ev - 'ry day with Je - sus Is sweet-er than the day be - fore;

Ev - 'ry day with Je - sus, I love Him more and more.

Je - sus saves and keeps me, And He's the One I'm wait - ing for.

Ev - 'ry day with Je - sus Is sweet-er than the day be - fore.

19 Blessed Be the Lord God Almighty

Revelation 4:8

B. F.

BOB FITTS

Fa - ther in heav-en, how___ we love___ You; We lift Your name___ in all the earth.___ May Your king - dom be es-tab-lished in___ our prais - es, As Your peo - ple de - clare Your might - y works.

20 Lord, Be Glorified

Philippians 1:20

B. K.

BOB KILPATRICK

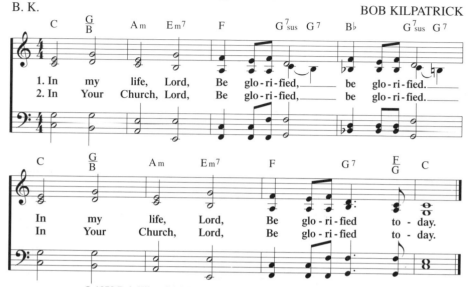

1. In my life, Lord, Be glo-ri-fied,_____ be glo-ri-fied._____
2. In Your Church, Lord, Be glo-ri-fied,_____ be glo-ri-fied._____

In my life, Lord, Be glo-ri-fied to-day.
In Your Church, Lord, Be glo-ri-fied to-day.

21 Bind Us Together

Ecclesiastes 4:12; Colossians 3:14

B. G.

BOB GILLMAN

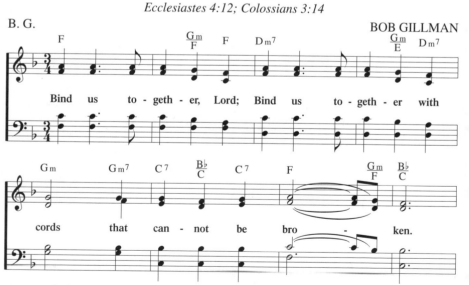

Bind us to-geth-er, Lord; Bind us to-geth-er with

cords that can-not be bro - ken.

22 This Is the Day

Psalm 118:24

L. G.

LES GARRETT

This is the day, this is the day That the Lord has made, that the Lord has made. We will re-joice, we will re-joice And be glad in it, and be glad in it. This is the day that the Lord has made. We will re-joice and be glad in it.

We Will Glorify

23

Revelation 15:14

T. P.

TWILA PARIS

1. We will glo - ri - fy the King of Kings; We will glo - ri - fy the Lamb. We will glo - ri - fy the Lord of Lords, Who is the great I AM.
2. Lord Je - ho - vah reigns in maj - es - ty; We will bow be - fore His throne. We will wor - ship Him in righ - teous - ness; We will wor - ship Him a - lone.
3. He is Lord of heav - en, Lord of earth; He is Lord of all who live. He is Lord a - bove the u - ni - verse; All praise to Him we give.
4. Hal - le - lu - jah to the King of Kings; Hal - le - lu - jah to the Lamb. Hal - le - lu - jah to the Lord of Lords, Who is the great I AM.

24   I Come to the Cross

B. B. and B. S.

BILL BATSTONE
and BOB SOMMA

I come to the cross seek-ing mer - cy and grace; I come to the cross where You died in my place. Out of my weak - ness and in - to Your strength; Hum - bly I come to the cross.

25 Turn Your Eyes upon Jesus

Hebrews 12:2

H. H. L. and KEN BIBLE

HELEN H. LEMMEL

1. Turn your eyes up - on Je - sus, Look full in His won - der - ful face, And the things of earth will grow strange - ly dim In the light of His glo - ry and grace.

2. Turn your eyes up - on Je - sus, Take hold of His pow - er - ful hand, He will lift you up in His might - y love, In the strength of your God you can stand.

More of You

GLORIA GAITHER

WILLIAM J. GAITHER
and GARY S. PAXTON

More of You, more of You; I've had all but what I need– just more of You. Of things I've had my fill, And yet I hun-ger still, Emp-ty and bare, Lord, hear my prayer for more of You.

27 All the Glory Belongs to Jesus

Revelation 5:12

GLORIA GAITHER

WILLIAM J. GAITHER

All the glo - ry be-longs to Je - sus.

All the praise be - longs to Him.

All that I am or ev - er hope to be,

All the glo - ry be - longs to Him.

Center of My Joy

28

GLORIA GAITHER

WILLIAM J. GAITHER and
RICHARD SMALLWOOD

Je - sus, You're the cen - ter of my joy,

All that's good and per - fect comes from You;

You're the heart of my con - tent - ment, hope for all I do,

Je - sus, You're the cen - ter of my joy.

29 Almighty

Revelation 4:8

W. W.

WAYNE WATSON

Al - might - y, most Ho - ly God;

Faith-ful thro' the a - ges. Al - might - y, most Ho - ly Lord;

Glo - ri-ous Al - might - y

God. God.

Sovereign Lord

30

T. F.

TOM FETTKE

Sov-'reign Lord, Sov-'reign Lord, We ex-alt Your ho-ly name, Sov-'reign Lord. Cre-a-tor, Re-deem-er, the King of Kings a-dored. Praise Your name, praise Your ho-ly name, Sov-'reign Lord.

31 Kingdom Prayer

Matthew 5:3-12

D. A.

DAN ADLER

32 Find Us Faithful

J. M.

JON MOHR

O may all who come be - hind___ us find us faith - ful;___

___ May the fire of our de - vo - tion light their___

way.___ May the foot - prints that we leave___

lead them to be - lieve,___ And the lives we live in -

spire them to o - bey. O may all who come be - hind us find us faith - ful.

I Will Be Christ to You

33

M. P.

MARTY PARKS

I will be Christ to you, I will be Christ to you; I'll be His hands to do what I can, Be-cause He has loved me, too— I will be Christ to you.

34 Arise, Shine

Isaiah 60:1

S. U. & J. R.

STEVEN URSPRINGER
and JAY ROBINSON

A - rise, shine, for thy light is come. A - rise, shine, for thy light is come. And the glo-ry of the Lord is ris-en, The glo-ry of the Lord is come, The

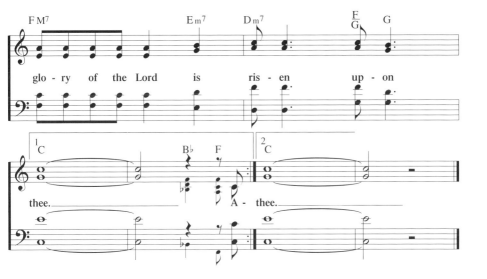

Hallelujah! Praise the Lamb 35

P. T., D. T.
& G. M.

PAM THUM, DAWN THOMAS
and GARY MCSPADDEN

36

Holy Spirit,
Thou Art Welcome

D. R. & D. H.

DOTTIE RAMBO
and DAVID HUNTSINGER

Every Moment of Every Day 37

N. J. C.

NORMAN J. CLAYTON

38 I Will Call upon the Lord

2 Samuel 22:47; Psalm 18:3

M. O'S.

MICHAEL O'SHIELDS

39   Be Still and Know

Psalm 46:10; Exodus 15:26; Psalm 56:4

Adapted

Unknown

Arranged by Lyndell Leatherman

Spirit of the Living God

Acts 4:31

D. I.

DANIEL IVERSON

Spir - it of the liv - ing God, fall fresh on me.

Spir - it of the liv - ing God, fall fresh on me.

Melt me, mold me, fill me, use me.

Spir - it of the liv - ing God, fall fresh on me.

41 As the Deer

Psalm 42:1

M. J. N.   MARTIN J. NYSTROM

1. As the deer pant-eth for the wa-ter, So my soul long-eth af - ter Thee; You a - lone are my heart's de - sire, And I long to wor - ship Thee. You a - lone are my strength, my shield, To You a - lone may my

2. I want You more than gold or sil - ver, On - ly You can sat - is - fy; You a - lone are the real Joy Giv - er, And the Ap - ple of my eye.

3. You're my Friend and You are my Broth - er, E - ven though You are a King; I love You more than an - y oth - er, So much more than an - y - thing.

spir - it yield;_____ You a - lone are my
heart's de - sire,___ And I long to wor - ship Thee.

Come, Holy Spirit   42

WILLIAM J. and
GLORIA GAITHER

WILLIAM J. GAITHER

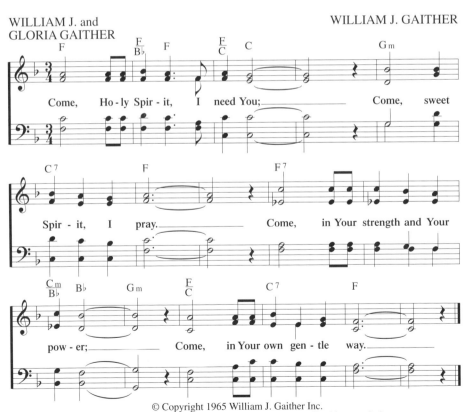

Come, Ho - ly Spir - it, I need You;_____ Come, sweet
Spir - it, I pray._____ Come, in Your strength and Your
pow - er;___ Come, in Your own gen - tle way.___

43   Desire of My Heart

M. P.

MARTY PARKS

O De-sire of my heart, O De-light of my soul; You fill me com-plete - ly, You make my life whole. You sur-round me with joy by the love on - ly You im - part: I will praise You for -

ev - er _____ O De-sire of my heart.

My Wonderful Lord 44

H. L.

HALDOR LILLENAS

My won-der-ful Lord, my won-der-ful Lord, By an-gels and

ser-aphs in heav-en a-dored. I bow at Thy shrine, My

Sav-ior di-vine, My won-der-ful, won-der-ful Lord. _____

45   Shout to the North

M. S.

MARTIN SMITH

1. Men of faith, rise up and sing of the great and glo - rious King, You are strong when you feel weak in your bro - ken - ness com - plete.

2. Rise up, wo - men of the truth, stand and sing to bro - ken hearts, Who can know the heal - ing pow'r of our awe - some King of love.

3. Rise up Church with bro - ken wings, fill this place with songs a - gain Of our God Who reigns on high, by His grace a - gain we'll fly.

CHORUS
*(We will) Shout to the north and the south,

*optional

46 Soon and Very Soon

Revelation 21:1-4

A. C.

ANDRAE CROUCH

1,4. Soon and ver - y soon,____ we are going to see the King!____
2. No more cry - ing there–____ we are going to see the King!____
3. No more dy - ing there–____ we are going to see the King!____

Soon and ver - y soon,____ we are going to see the King!____
No more cry - ing there–____ we are going to see the King!____
No more dy - ing there–____ we are going to see the King!____

Soon and ver - y soon,____ we are going to see the King!____
No more cry - ing there–____ we are going to see the King!____ Hal-le-
No more dy - ing there–____ we are going to see the King!____

lu - jah! Hal-le-lu - jah!____ We're going to see the King!

Coming Again 47

I Thess. 4:16-17; I John 3:2; Rev. 1:7

M. L.   MOSIE LISTER

1. Je - sus is com - ing; Je - sus is com - ing;
2. In clouds of glo - ry, Bright clouds of glo - ry,
3. We'll rise to meet Him, Rise up to meet Him;
4. We shall be like Him; We shall be like Him;
5. Oh, hal - le - lu - jah! Oh, hal - le - lu - jah!

Je - sus is com - ing. He's com - ing a - gain.
In clouds of glo - ry He's com - ing a - gain.
We'll rise to meet Him. He's com - ing a - gain.
We shall be like Him. He's com - ing a - gain.
Oh, hal - le - lu - jah! He's com - ing a - gain.

48 There's Something About that Name

WILLIAM J. and
GLORIA GAITHER

WILLIAM J. GAITHER

Lyrics:

Je - sus, Je - sus, Je - sus! There's just some - thing a - bout that name! Mas - ter, Sav - ior, Je - sus! Like the fra - grance af - ter the rain. Je - sus, Je - sus, Je - sus! Let all heav - en and

earth pro-claim:___ Kings and king-doms___ will all pass a-

way, But there's some-thing a - bout that name!___

Holy Savior

49

M. L.

MOSIE LISTER

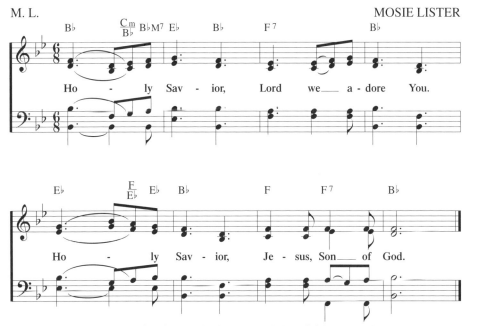

Ho - ly Sav - ior, Lord we__ a-dore You.

Ho - ly Sav - ior, Je - sus, Son__ of God.

50 Holy Ground

Exodus 3:5

G. D.

GERON DAVIS

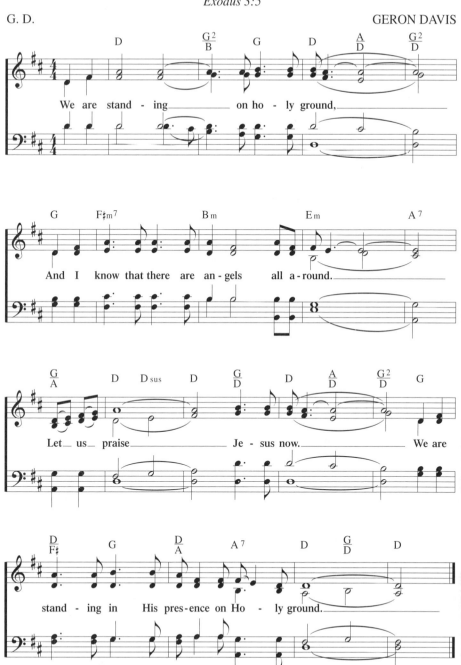

We are stand - ing ___ on ho - ly ground, ___

And I know that there are an - gels all a - round. ___

Let ___ us ___ praise ___ Je - sus now. ___ We are

stand - ing in His pres - ence on Ho - ly ground. ___

Soften My Heart

51

G. K.

GRAHAM KENDRICK

Soft-en my heart, Lord, soft-en my heart;

From all in - dif - f'rence set me a - part.

To feel Your com-pas - sion, to weep with Your tears;

Come soft-en my heart, O Lord, soft-en my heart.

52

Holy, You Are Holy

B. M.

BRUCE WICKERSHEIM

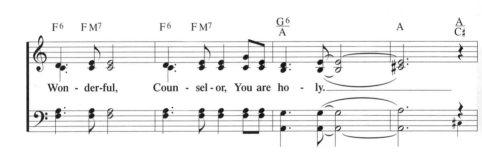

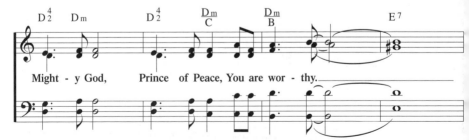

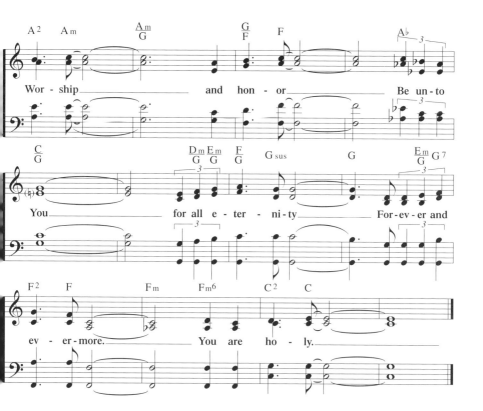

Father, I Adore You 53

T. C. S.

TERRYE COELHO STROM

1. Fa - ther, I a - dore You, Lay my life be - fore You. How I love You!
2. Je - sus, I a - dore You, Lay my life be - fore You. How I love You!
3. Spir - it, I a - dore You, Lay my life be - fore You. How I love You!

54 Let the Beauty of Jesus Be Seen in Me

ALBERT ORSBORN

TOM JONES

Let the beau - ty of Je - sus be seen in me—

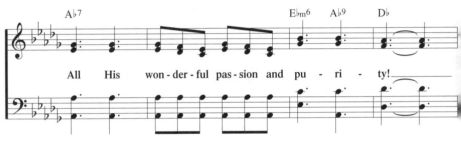

All His won - der - ful pas - sion and pu - ri - ty!

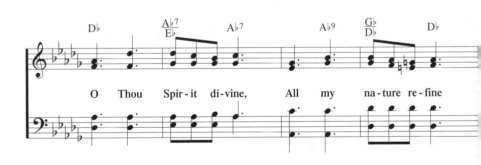

O Thou Spir - it di - vine, All my na - ture re - fine

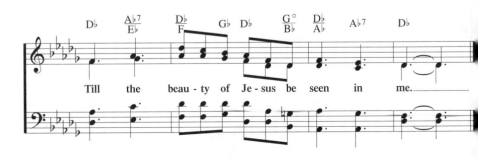

Till the beau - ty of Je - sus be seen in me.

Something Beautiful

55

GLORIA GAITHER

WILLIAM J. GAITHER

Some - thing beau - ti - ful, some - thing good;

All my con - fu - sion He un - der - stood.

All I had to of - fer Him was bro ken - ness and

strife, But He made some - thing beau - ti - ful of my life.

56 Be Exalted, O God

Psalm 57:9-11

Adapted by B. C.

BRENT CHAMBERS

57 Bless His Holy Name

Psalm 103:1-2

Adapted by A. C.

ANDRAE CROUCH

Worthy, You Are Worthy

Revelation 5:12

58

D. M.

DON MOEN

1. Wor - thy, You are wor - thy; King of
2. Ho - ly, You are ho - ly; King of
3. Je - sus, You are Je - sus; King of

Kings, Lord of Lords, You are wor - thy.
Kings, Lord of Lords, You are ho - ly.
Kings, Lord of Lords, You are Je - sus.

Wor - thy, You are wor - thy; King of
Ho - ly, You are ho - ly; King of
Je - sus, You are Je - sus; King of

Kings, Lord of Lords, I wor - ship You.
Kings, Lord of Lords, I wor - ship You.
Kings, Lord of Lords, I wor - ship You.

59 God Is Great, God Is Good

Psalm 136:1

M. P.

MARTY PARKS

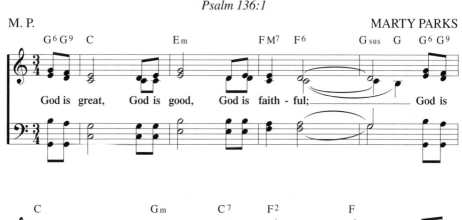

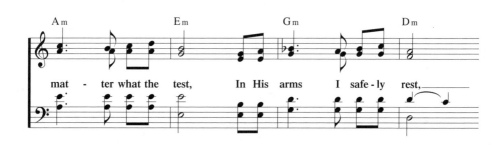

Cares Chorus

I Peter 5:7

K. W.

KELLY WILLARD

I cast all my cares up-on You. I lay all of my bur-dens down at Your feet. And an-y time that I don't know what to do, I will cast all my cares up-on You.

61 Bless That Wonderful Name

Traditional and KEN BIBLE

Traditional
Arranged by Tom Fettke

1. Bless that won-der-ful name of Je-sus. Bless that won-der-ful name of Je-sus. Bless that won-der-ful name of Je-sus.
2. Might-y is the name of Je-sus. Ho-ly is the name of Je-sus. Glo-rious is the name of Je-sus.
3. Wor-thy is the name of Je-sus. Won-der-ful the name of Je-sus. Son of God is He of my Je-sus.
4. Praise that won-der-ful name of Je-sus. Praise that won-der-ful name of Je-sus. Praise that won-der-ful name of Je-sus.

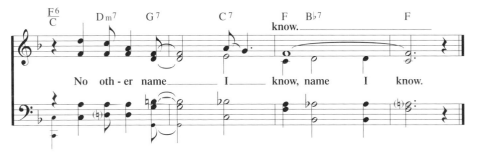

Jesus, Name Above All Names 62

N. H.

NAIDA HEARN

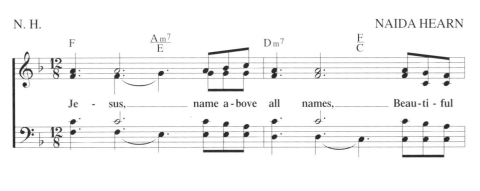

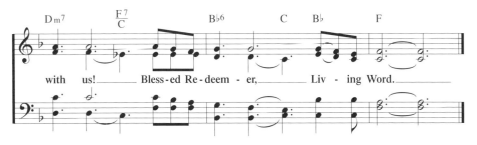

63 Give Thanks

Psalm 136:1

H. S.

HENRY SMITH

Give thanks with a grate-ful heart;— Give thanks to the

Ho - ly One;— Give thanks—— be-cause He's giv-en Je - sus Christ, His—

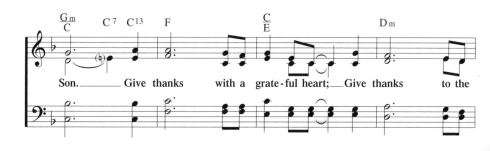

Son.——— Give thanks with a grate-ful heart;—Give thanks to the

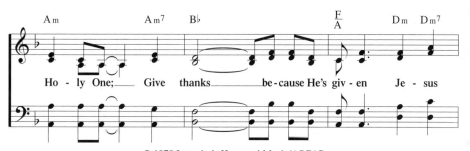

Ho - ly One;— Give thanks——— be-cause He's giv - en Je - sus

64 Change My Heart, O God

Psalm 51:10

E. E.

EDDIE ESPINOSA

Mold me and make me, this is what I pray.

Sanctuary
I Corinthians 6:19-20

65

J. T. and R. S.

JOHN THOMPSON
and RANDY SCRUGGS

Lord, pre-pare me to be a sanc-tu-ar-y, pure and ho-ly, tried and true; With thanks-giv-ing, I'll be a liv-ing sanc-tu-ar-y for You.

66 Come Just As You Are

J. S.

JOSEPH SABOLICK

1. Come just as you are; Hear the Spir - it call.
2. Come just as you are; Hear the Spir - it call.

Come just as you are; Come and see, come, re - ceive;
Come just as you are; Come, re - ceive Christ, the King;

Come and live for - ev - er. Life e - ver - last - ing, and
Come and live for -

strength for to - day; Taste the Liv - ing Wa - ter, and

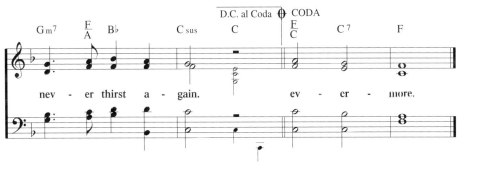

nev - er thirst a - gain. ev - er - more.

Into My Heart

67

Revelation 3:20

H. D. C.

HARRY D. CLARKE

In - to my heart, in - to my heart, Come in - to my

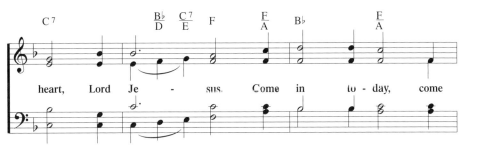

heart, Lord Je - sus. Come in to - day, come

in to stay– Come in - to my heart, Lord Je - sus.

68   Go Light Your World

Matthew 5:14

C. R.

CHRIS RICE

1. There is a can - dle in ev - 'ry soul,_____ Some burn-ing
2. Frus - trat - ed broth - er, see how he's tried to Light his own
3. We are a fam - 'ly whose hearts are blaz - ing. Let's raise our

bright-ly, some dark and cold._____ There is a Spir - it who brings a
can - dle some oth - er way._____ See now your sis - ter, she's been robbed and
can - dles— light up the sky!_____ Pray to our Fath - er in the name of

fire,_____ Ig - nites a can - dle and makes His home.
lied to, Still holds a can - dle with-out a flame. Car-ry your
Je - sus; Make us a bea - con in dark - est times.

can - dle, run to the dark - ness, Seek out the hope - less, con -fused and

The Servant Song 69

R. G.

RICHARD GILLARD

1,6. Broth - er, let me be your ser - vant, Let me be as Christ to you;
2. We are pil - grims on a jour - ney; We are broth - ers on the road.
3. I will hold the Christ - light for you In the night - time of your fear;
4. I will weep when you are weep - ing; When you laugh, I'll laugh with you.
5. When we sing to God in heav - en, We shall find such har - mo - ny,

Pray that I may have the grace to Let you be my ser - vant too.
We are here to help each oth - er Walk the mile and bear the load.
I will hold my hand out to you, Speak the peace you long to hear.
I will share your joy and sor - row Till we've seen this jour - ney thro'.
Born of all we've known to - geth - er Of Christ's love and ag - o - ny.

70   I Have Decided to Follow Jesus

Matthew 16:24

Anonymous

Folk Melody from India
Arranged by Lyndell Leatherman

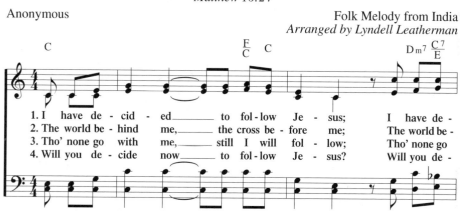

1. I have de - cid - ed_____ to fol - low Je - sus; I have de -
2. The world be - hind me,_____ the cross be - fore me; The world be -
3. Tho' none go with me,_____ still I will fol - low; Tho' none go
4. Will you de - cide now_____ to fol - low Je - sus? Will you de -

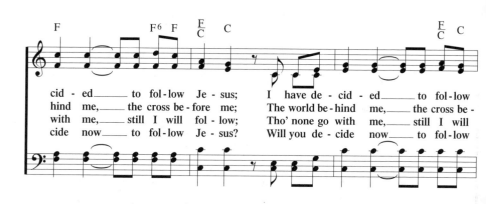

cid - ed_____ to fol - low Je - sus; I have de - cid - ed_____ to fol - low
hind me,_____ the cross be - fore me; The world be - hind me,_____ the cross be -
with me,_____ still I will fol - low; Tho' none go with me,_____ still I will
cide now_____ to fol - low Je - sus? Will you de - cide now_____ to fol - low

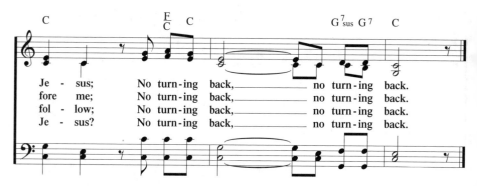

Je - sus; No turn - ing back,_____ no turn - ing back.
fore me; No turn - ing back,_____ no turn - ing back.
fol - low; No turn - ing back,_____ no turn - ing back.
Je - sus? No turn - ing back,_____ no turn - ing back.

For God So Loved the World 71

John 3:16

FRANCES TOWNSEND

ALFRED B. SMITH

For God so loved the world, He gave His on-ly
Son To die on Cal-v'ry's tree, from sin to set me
free. Some day He's com-ing back; what glo-ry that will
be! Won - der-ful His love to me.

72 Emmanuel

Matthew 1:23

B. M.

BOB MCGEE

Em - man - u - el,_____ Em - man - u - el,_____

His name is called_____ Em - man - u - el:_____

God with us,_____ re - vealed in us!

His name is called_____ Em - man - u - el.

Blessed Be the Name of the Lord 73

D. M.

DON MOEN

Bless-ed be the name of the Lord, He is wor-thy to be praised and a-dored; So we lift up ho-ly hands in one ac-cord, Sing-ing, "Bless-ed be the name, bless-ed be the name, Bless-ed be the name of the Lord!"

74 Majesty

J. H.

JACK HAYFORD

75 God Can Do Anything but Fail

Luke 1:37

I. F. S.

IRA F. STANPHILL

God can do an-y-thing, an-y-thing, an-y-thing; God can do an-y-thing but fail. He can save, He can keep, He can cleanse, and He will; God can do an-y-thing but fail. He's the Al-pha and O-me-ga, the be-gin-ning and the end; He's the

fair-est of ten thou-sand to my soul._____ God can do an-y-thing,

an-y-thing, an-y-thing; God can do an-y-thing but fail.

Lord, Lay Some Soul upon My Heart

76

LEON TUCKER

IRA D. SANKEY

Lord, lay some soul up - on my heart And love that soul thro' me;_____ And

may I glad - ly do my part To win that soul for Thee._____

77 Behold, I Am the Lord

Jeremiah 32:27

D. W.

DAN WHITTEMORE

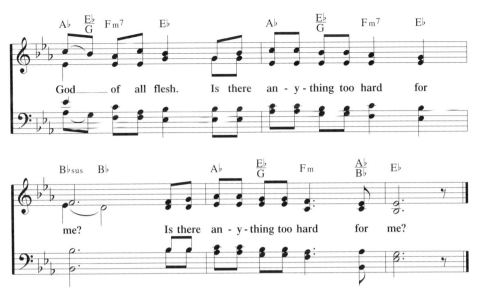

God____ of all flesh. Is there an-y-thing too hard for
me? Is there an-y-thing too hard for me?

God Is So Good

Psalm 136:1

78

1. God is so good, God is so good,
2. He cares for me, He cares for me,
3. I'll do His will, I'll do His will,
4. He is my Lord, He is my Lord,

God is so good, He's so good to me!
He cares for me, He's so good to me!
I'll do His will He's so good to me!
He is my Lord, He's so good to me!

79 When We Talk to Him

K. B.

KEN BIBLE

When we talk to Him_____ He will hear___ us;_____
_____ He will lis - ten to all that we say._____
_____ For the Lord of all is our clos - est
friend; He is with___ us as now we pray.___

To Worship You

80

KEN BIBLE

TOM FETTKE and
RICHARD KINGSMORE

1. As we come to - day to wor - ship You,
2. As we came to - day to wor - ship You,

Lord, we give our - selves to wor - ship You.
We will live this week to wor - ship You.

With our thoughts, with our words, with our lives, with our

love, We wor - ship, We wor - ship You.

81 The Love of Christ

Ephesians 3:14-19

M. P.

MARTY PARKS

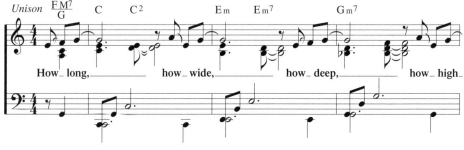

How long, how wide, how deep, how high

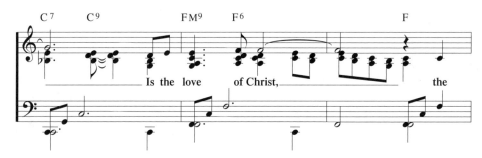

Is the love of Christ, the

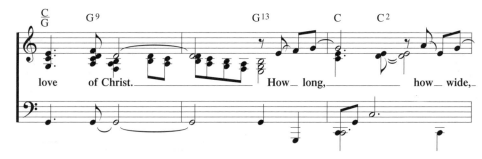

love of Christ. How long, how wide,

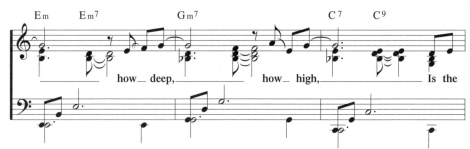

how deep, how high, Is the

82   Let There Be an Anointing

J. H.

JACK HAYFORD

1. Let there be an a-noint-ing of the Spir - it.
2. Let there be a dis-play-ing of Thy glo - ry.
3. Let there be an ex-alt-ing of Christ Je - sus.

Let there be an out-pour-ing of Thy pow'r.
Let there be a re-veal-ing of Thy grace.
Let there be an un-fold-ing of the Word.

Let there be an o-ver-flow-ing of the love of God,
Let there be an un-der-stand-ing of Thy will and way,
Let the truth bring lib-er-ty of life and health,

That Thy name be mag-ni-fied this hour.
That Thy king-dom come with-in this place.
That Thy name be mag-ni-fied as Lord.

In the Name of the Lord

John 14:13

83

S. P. H., P. M. and G. G.

SANDI PATTI HELVERING,
PHILL MCHUGH and GLORIA GAITHER

There is strength in the name of the Lord.

There is pow'r in the name of the Lord.

There is hope in the name of the Lord.

Bless-ed is He who comes in the name of the Lord.

84   God Said It, I Believe It, That Settles It

S. R. A. and GENE BRAUN

STEPHEN R. ADAMS

God said it and I be-lieve it, And that set-tles it for me! God said it and I be-live it, And that set-tles it for me! Though some may doubt that His Word is true, I've cho-sen to be-lieve it; now how a-bout you? God

said it and I be-lieve it, And that set-tles it for me!

Praise Him

85

Traditional
Arranged by Lyndell Leatherman

Praise___ Him, praise___ Him,___ Praise Him in the morn-ing, Praise Him at the noon-time, Praise___ Him,___ praise___ Him,___ Praise Him when the sun goes down.

86 Jesus Is Lord of All

Philippians 2:9-11

W. J. and GLORIA GAITHER

WILLIAM J. GAITHER

1. All my to - mor - rows, all my past; Je - sus is
2. All of my con - flicts, all my thoughts; Je - sus is
3. All of my long - ings, all my dreams; Je - sus is

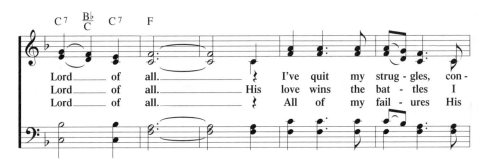

Lord_____ of all._____ I've quit my strug - gles, con -
Lord_____ of all._____ His love wins the bat - tles I
Lord_____ of all._____ All of my fail - ures His

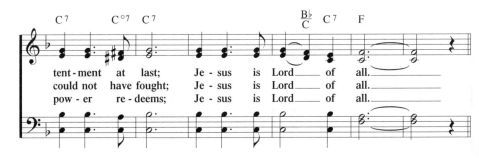

tent - ment at last; Je - sus is Lord_____ of all._____
could not have fought; Je - sus is Lord_____ of all._____
pow - er re - deems; Je - sus is Lord_____ of all._____

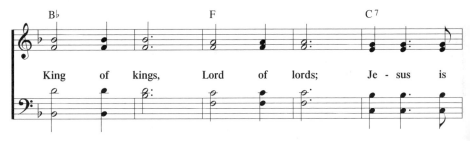

King of kings, Lord of lords; Je - sus is

Lord of all. All my pos-sess-ions and all my life; Je-sus is Lord of all.

There Is No God like You 87

Jeremiah 10:6-7

D. W.

DAN WHITTEMORE

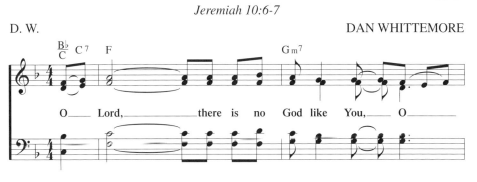

O Lord, there is no God like You, O

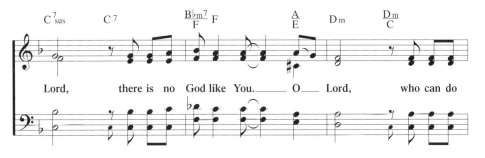

Lord, there is no God like You. O Lord, who can do

Let There Be Glory and Honor and Praises

88

Revelation 5:12

J. G. and E. G.

JAMES and ELIZABETH GREENELSH

89 To Him Who Sits on the Throne

Revelation 5:13

D. G.

DEBBYE GRAAFSMA

ev - er,_____ Be bless - ing and glo - ry and
hon - or and pow - er for - ev - er!_____

Jesus, I Love You 90

O. S.

OTIS SKILLINGS

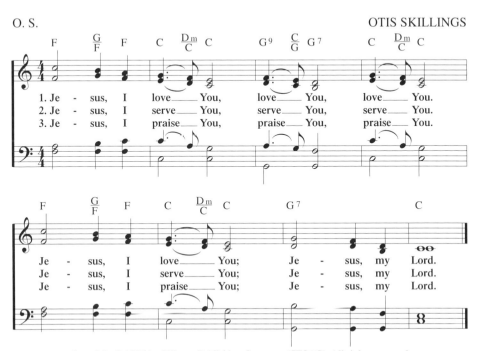

1. Je - sus, I love____ You, love____ You, love____ You.
2. Je - sus, I serve____ You, serve____ You, serve____ You.
3. Je - sus, I praise____ You, praise____ You, praise____ You.

Je - sus, I love_____ You; Je - sus, my Lord.
Je - sus, I serve_____ You; Je - sus, my Lord.
Je - sus, I praise_____ You; Je - sus, my Lord.

91 I Sing Praises

Psalm 96:1-4

T. M.

TERRY MACALMON

1. I sing prais - es to Your name, O___ Lord,
2. I give glo - ry to Your name, O___ Lord,

Prais - es to Your name, O___ Lord, For Your
Glo - ry to Your name, O___ Lord, For Your

name is great and great - ly to be praised;
name is great and great - ly to be praised;

I sing prais - es to Your name, O___ Lord,
I give glo - ry to Your name, O___ Lord,

Lord, We Praise You 92

O. S.

OTIS SKILLINGS

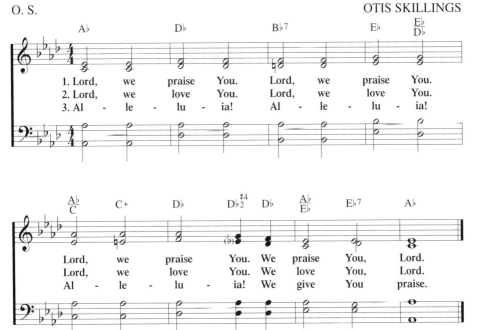

93

Grace Alone

Ephesians 2:8-9

S. W. B. and J. N.

SCOTT WESLEY BROWN
and JEFF NELSON

1. Ev - 'ry prom-ise we can make, Ev - 'ry prayer and step of faith,
2. Ev - 'ry soul we long to reach, Ev - 'ry heart we hope to teach,

Ev - 'ry dif - f'rence we will make, is on - ly by His
Ev - 'ry - where we share His peace, is on - ly by His

grace. Ev - 'ry moun-tain we will climb, Ev - 'ry ray of
grace. Ev - 'ry lov - ing word we say, Ev - 'ry tear we

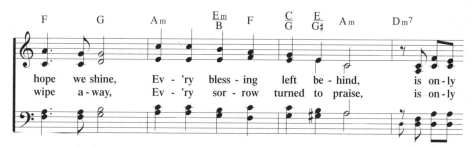

hope we shine, Ev - 'ry bless - ing left be - hind, is on - ly
wipe a - way, Ev - 'ry sor - row turned to praise, is on - ly

by_____ His grace. Grace a - lone, which God sup - plies,
by_____ His grace.

Strength un - known He will pro - vide. Christ in us,_____

_____ our cor - ner - stone, We will go forth in grace a - lone.

You Are My All in All 94

D. J.

DENNIS JERNIGAN

1. You are my strength when I am weak; You are the
2. Tak - ing my sin, my cross, my shame; Ris - ing a -

I Give All to You

L. H.

LARNELLE HARRIS

1. I give all my ser-vice to You,_____ I give all my
2. I give all my prob-lems to You,_____ I give all my
3. I give all my fam-'ly to You,_____ I give all my
4. I give all my fu-ture to You,_____ I give all my
5. I give all my wor-ship to You,_____ I give all my

ser - vice to You;_____ No mat-ter the cost_____ or
prob-lems to You;_____ No mat-ter the cost_____ or
fam - 'ly to You;_____ No mat-ter the cost_____ or
fu - ture to You;_____ No mat-ter the cost_____ or
wor - ship to You;_____ No mat-ter the cost_____ or

what oth-ers do,_____ I give all my ser - vice to You.
what oth-ers do,_____ I give all my prob - lems to You.
what oth-ers do,_____ I give all my fam - 'ly to You.
what oth-ers do,_____ I give all my fu - ture to You.
what oth-ers do,_____ I give all my wor - ship to You.

22

96 More Love, More Power

J. D. H.

JUDE DEL HIERRO

97

Jesus Is Lord

Romans 10:10; Philippians 2:9-11

ED SEABOUGH

OTIS SKILLINGS

1. With my heart I be - lieve, Je - sus Christ is Lord;
2. With my lips I con - fess, Je - sus Christ is Lord;

And that Je - sus rose a - gain, Je - sus Christ is Lord.
And I, too, shall live a - gain, Je - sus Christ is Lord.

Je - sus is Lord, Lord of my life; Je - sus is Lord,

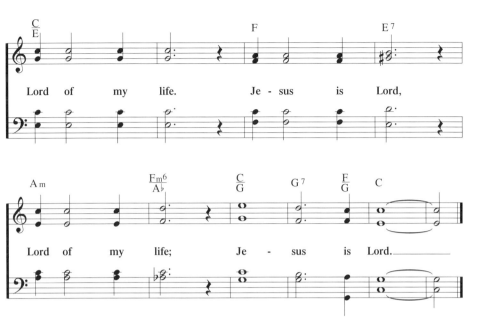

Lord of my life. Je - sus is Lord,

Lord of my life; Je - sus is Lord.

I Live by Faith

98

Galatians 2:20

Adapted

C. C. DUNBAR

I live by faith in Him who died; With Him I have been cru-ci-fied.

I live and yet it is not I, But Christ who lives in me.

99 Our God Reigns

Isaiah 52:7

L. E. S.

LEONARD E. SMITH, JR.

1. How love-ly on the moun-tains are the feet of them
2. He had no state - ly form; He had no maj - es - ty.
3. Out from the tomb He came with grace and maj - es - ty.

Who bring good news, good news. An-nounc-ing
That we should be drawn to Him. He was de-
He is a - live! He is a - live! God loves us

peace, pro - claim - ing news of hap - pi - ness; Our God
spised, and we took no ac - count of Him; Yet now He
so— see here His hands, His feet, His side. Yes, we

reigns; our God reigns!
reigns with the Most High! Our God
know He is a - live!

Thy Word

100

Psalm 119:105

Adapted by AMY GRANT

MICHAEL W. SMITH

101 Gentle Shepherd

Psalm 23:1-3

W. J. G. and GLORIA GAITHER

WILLIAM J. GAITHER

lead us._____ For we need you to help us find our way._____

Just a Closer Walk with Thee 102

Unknown

1. I am weak but Thou art strong; _____ Je - sus,
2. Thro' this world of toil and snares, _____ If I
3. When my fee - ble life is o'er, _____ Time for
Refrain: Just a clos - er walk with Thee– _____ *Grant it,*

keep me from all wrong; _____ I'll be sat - is - fied as
fal - ter, Lord, who cares? _____ Who with me my bur - den
me will be no more; _____ Guide me gen - tly, safe - ly
Je - sus, is my plea. _____ *Dai - ly walk - ing close to*

Refrain D.C.

long _____ As I walk, let me walk close to Thee.
shares? _____ None but Thee, dear__ Lord, none but Thee.
o'er _____ To Thy king - dom shore, to Thy shore.
Thee– _____ *Let it be, dear__ Lord, let it be.*

103 We Bring the Sacrifice of Praise

Hebrews 13:15

K. D.

KIRK DEARMAN

We bring the sac-ri-fice of praise_____ in - to the house of the Lord,_____ house of the Lord. And we of - fer up to You_____ the sac-ri-fi - ces of thanks-giv-ing, And we of - fer up to You_____ the sac-ri-fi - ces of joy!

Surely the Presence of the Lord Is in This Place

104

Genesis 28:16

L. W.

LANNY WOLFE

Sure - ly the pres-ence of the Lord is in this place; I can feel His might-y pow - er and His grace. I can hear the brush of an-gels' wings, I see glo - ry on each face; Sure - ly the pres - ence of the Lord is in this place.

105 In His Time

Ecclesiastes 3:11

D. B.

DIANE BALL

1. In His time (in His time), in His time (in His
2. In Your time (in Your time), in Your time (in Your

time); He makes all things beau - ti - ful in His
time); You make all things beau - ti - ful in Your

time (in His time). Lord, please show me ev - 'ry
time (in Your time). Lord, my life to You I

day As You're teach - ing me Your way, That You
bring: May each song I have to sing Be to

do just what You say In Your time (in Your time).
you a love-ly thing in Your time (in Your time).

Isn't the Love of Jesus Something Wonderful   106

J. W. P.

JOHN W. PETERSON

Is-n't the love of Je - sus some-thing won - der - ful,____ won - der - ful, won - der - ful! O is - n't the love of Je - sus some-thing won - der-ful!_____ Won-der-ful it is to me.

107 He Is Able

2 Corinthians 9:8

R. N. and G. F.

RORY NOLAND and
GREG FERGUSON

He is a-ble, more than a-ble to ac-com-plish what con-cerns me to-day. He is a-ble, more than a-ble to han-dle an-y-thing that comes my way. He is a-ble, more than a-ble to do much more than I could ev-er dream, He is

Praise the Name of Jesus 108

R. H.

ROY HICKS, JR.

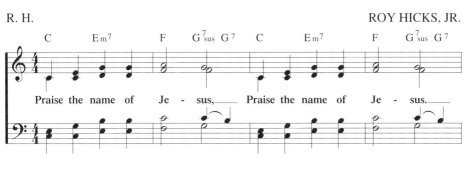

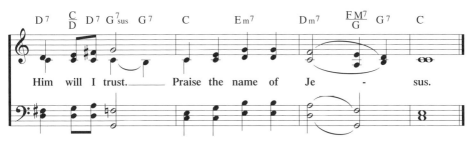

109 Lift Up the Cross

John 12:32

D. A. and N. A.

DENNIS and NAN ALLEN

Lift up the cross!_____ Lift up the cross,_____ 'Til ev - 'ry
eye has_ seen the Lamb of Cal - va - ry. Lift up the
cross!_____ Lift up the cross!_____ Ex - alt the Son of God who_
died, Take up His cross and lift it_ high, 'Til ev - 'ry

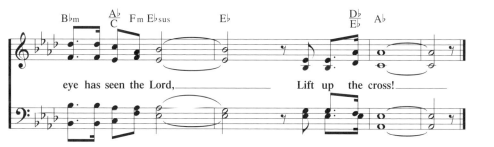

eye has seen the Lord,_____ Lift up the cross!_____

With Eternity's Values in View 110

A. B. S.

ALFRED B. SMITH

With e - ter - ni - ty's val - ues in view, Lord;

With e - ter - ni - ty's val - ues in view–

May I do each day's work for Je - sus

With e - ter - ni - ty's val - ues in view._____

111 My Life Is in You, Lord

D. G.

DANIEL GARDNER

112   O the Glory of Your Presence

S. F.

STEVE FRY

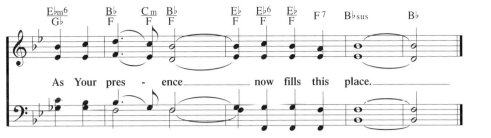

As Your pres - ence_____ now fills this place._____

Jesus, Your Name 113

C. C. and M. C.

CLAIRE CLONINGER
and MORRIS CHAPMAN

1. Je - sus, Your name_____ is pow - er; Je - sus, Your name__ is_____
2. Je - sus, Your name_____ is heal - ing; Je - sus, Your name__ gives__
3. Je - sus, Your name_____ is ho - ly; Je - sus, Your name__ brings_

might. Je - sus, Your name_____ will break ev - 'ry
sight. Je - sus, Your name_____ will free ev - 'ry
light. Je - sus, Your name_____ a - bove ev - 'ry

strong - hold; Je - sus, Your name_____ is life.
cap - tive; Je - sus, Your name_____ is life.
oth - er; Je - sus, Your name_____ is life.

114 Come, Let Us Worship and Bow Down

Psalm 95:6-7

Adapted by D. D.

DAVE DOHERTY

Come, let us wor-ship and bow down;
Let us kneel be-fore the Lord our God, our Mak - er.

Come, let us wor-ship and bow down;
Let us kneel be-fore the Lord our God, our Mak - er
For

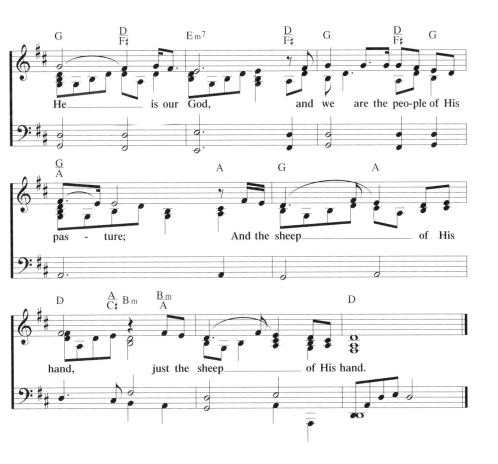

He _____ is our God, and we are the peo-ple of His
pas - ture; And the sheep _____ of His
hand, just the sheep _____ of His hand.

I Thank the Lord for You   115

Philippians 1:3-11

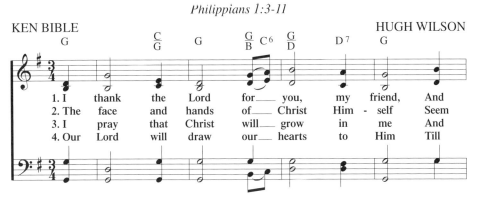

KEN BIBLE

HUGH WILSON

1. I thank the Lord for you, my friend, And
2. The face and hands of Christ Him - self Seem
3. I pray that Christ will grow in me And
4. Our Lord will draw our hearts to Him Till

I Believe the Answer's on the Way

116

Hebrews 10:35

M. D.

MERRILL DUNLOP

I be-lieve the an-swer's on the way;
Now by faith in Him a-lone I stand,

I be-lieve the Lord has heard me pray;___ "Cast not away your
Firm-ly held by His al-might-y hand;___ Ful-ly___ trust-ing

con - fi-dence," saith the Lord our God.___

in His prom-ise, praise the Lord!

117   Hosanna

C. T.

CARL TUTTLE

1. Ho - san - na, ho - san - na, Ho - san-na
2. Glo - ry, glo - ry, Glo - ry

in the high - est; Ho - san - na, ho -
to the King of Kings; Glo - ry,

san - na, Ho - san-na in the high - est.
glo - ry, Glo-ry to the King of Kings.

Lord, we lift up__ Your name,

With

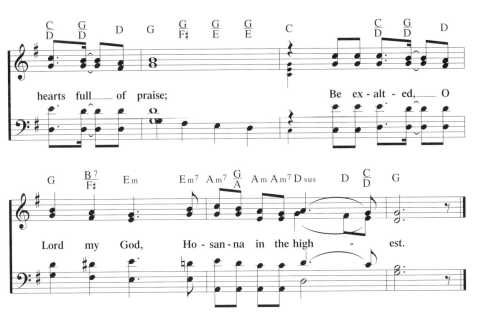

hearts full___ of praise; Be ex-alt-ed,___ O

Lord my God, Ho-san-na in the high - est.

O Come, Let Us Adore Him 118

Traditional

Attr. to JOHN F. WADE

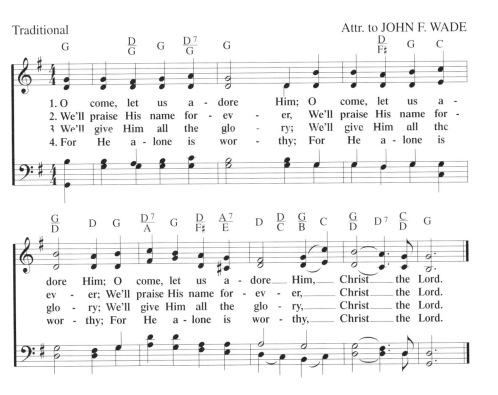

1. O   come, let   us   a - dore   Him; O   come, let   us   a -
2. We'll praise His name for - ev - er, We'll praise His name for-
3. We'll give Him   all   the   glo   -   ry; We'll give Him   all   the
4. For   He   a - lone   is   wor - thy; For   He   a - lone   is

dore Him; O come, let   us   a - dore___ Him,___ Christ___ the Lord.
ev - er; We'll praise His name for - ev - er,___ Christ___ the Lord.
glo - ry; We'll give Him   all   the   glo - ry,___ Christ___ the Lord.
wor - thy; For   He   a - lone   is   wor - thy,___ Christ___ the Lord.

119 I Can, I Will, I Do Believe

Traditional and ELIZA H. HAMILTON

Traditional and J. H. STOCKTON
Arranged by Lyndell Leatherman

I can, I will, I do be-lieve;___ I can, I will, I do be-lieve;___ I can, I will, I do be-lieve___ That Je - sus saves me now.___ He takes me as___ I am;___ He takes me as___ I am.___ He brings His free sal - va - tion to me, And takes me as I am.___

Lead Me to Some Soul Today 120

WILL H. HOUGHTON

WENDELL P. LOVELESS

Lead me to some soul to-day; Oh, teach me, Lord, just what to say;—

Friends of mine are lost in sin And can-not find their way.

Few there are who seem to care, And few there are who pray.

Melt my heart and fill my life, Give me one soul to-day.

121 I Stand in Awe

M. A.

MARK ALTROGGE

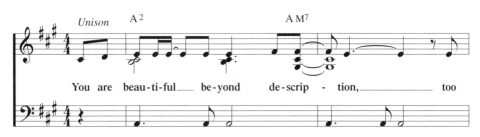

You are beau-ti-ful___ be-yond de-scrip - tion,_____ too

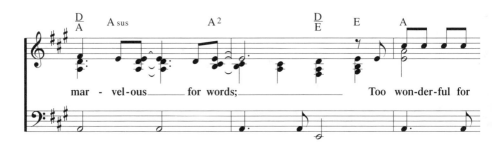

mar - vel-ous_____ for words;_____ Too won-der-ful for

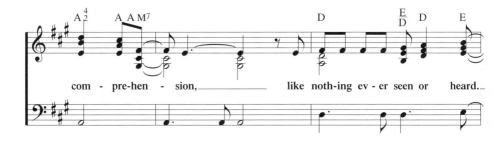

com - pre-hen - sion,_____ like noth-ing ev - er seen or heard.__

_____ Who can grasp Your in - fi-nite__ wis - dom?

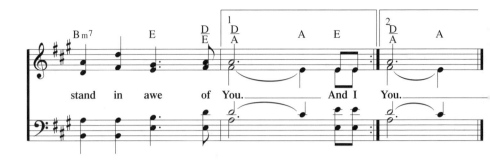

stand in awe of You. ___ And I ___ You. ___

122

Above All

Ephesians 1:18-23

L. L. & P. B.

LENNY LEBLANC
and PAUL BALOCHE

A-bove all pow - ers, a-bove all kings, A-bove all
(A-bove all) king - doms, a-bove all thrones, A-bove all

na - ture and all cre-at - ed things; A-bove all
won - ders the world has ev - er known; A-bove all

wis - dom and all the ways of man, ___ A-bove all
wealth ___ and trea - sures of the earth, ___

123   I Will Sing of the Mercies

Psalm 89:1

Adapted   Unknown
Arranged by David Cole

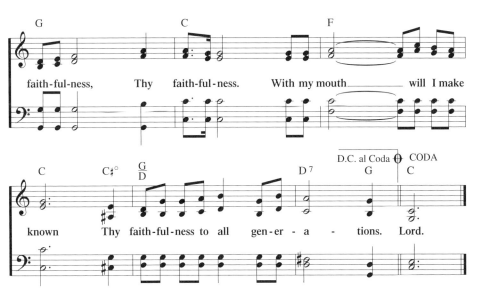

faith-ful-ness, Thy faith-ful-ness. With my mouth _____ will I make

known Thy faith-ful-ness to all gen-er - a - tions. Lord.

He Has Made Me Glad 124

Psalm 100:4

L. V. B.   LEONA VAN BRETHORST

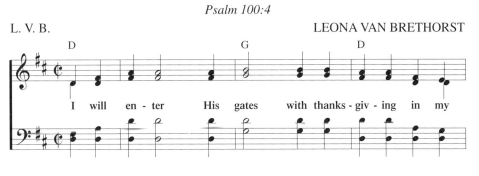

I will en - ter His gates with thanks - giv - ing in my

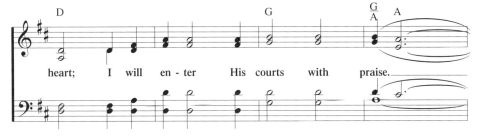

heart; I will en - ter His courts with praise.

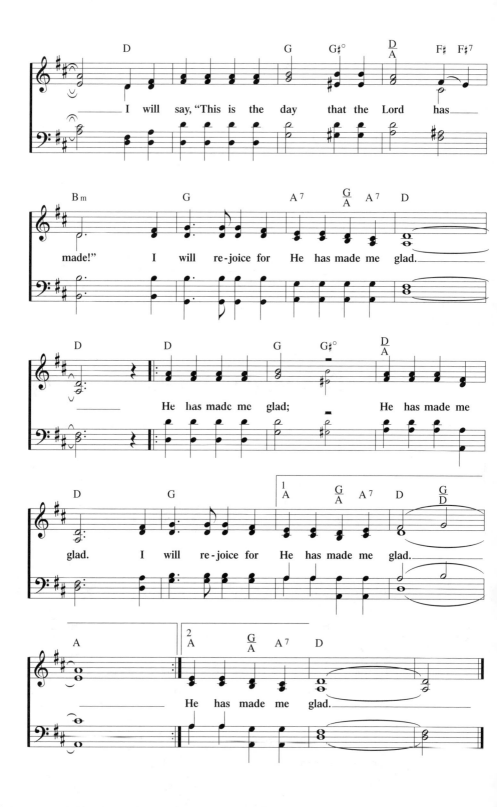

Dare to Run

125

Hebrews 12:1-3

H. M. & J. W. S.

HARLAN MOORE
and JOEL W. SMITH

Dare to run with our eyes fixed on Je - sus, Fol - low - ing the foot - steps of the One who's gone be - fore us. Dare to run in the pow - er of His Spir - it, Called to be vic - tors in a race al - read - y won; Dare to run.

126 Think About His Love

W. H.

WALT HARRAH

Think a-bout His love,_____ think a-bout His good - ness,

_____ Think a-bout His grace_____ that's bro't us through.

_____ For as high as the heav-ens a-bove,_____ so

great is the mea-sure of our Fa-ther's love._____

Great is the mea-sure of our Fa-ther's love.

Let Go and Let God Have His Way

127

H. D. C.

HARRY D. CLARKE

Let go and let God have His won-der-ful way; Let go and let God have His way. Your bur-dens will van-ish, your night turn to day; Let go and let God have His way.

128 I've Discovered the Way of Gladness

F. W. H.

FLOYD W. HAWKINS

I've dis-cov-ered the way of glad-ness; I've dis-cov-ered the way of joy; I've dis-cov-ered re-lief from sad-ness— 'Tis a hap-pi-ness with-out al-loy. I've dis-cov-ered the fount of bless-ing; I've dis-cov-ered the liv-ing Word_____ 'Twas the

great-est of all dis - cov - er - ies When I found Je-sus, my Lord.

Learning to Lean 129

J. S.

JOHN STALLINGS

Learn - ing to lean,_____ learn - ing to lean, I'm

learn - ing to lean on Je - sus.____

Find - ing more pow - er than I'd ev - er dreamed, I'm

learn - ing to lean on Je - sus.

130 Lamb of God

T. P.

TWILA PARIS

1. Your on - ly Son____ no sin to hide, But You have
2. Your gift of love____ they cru - ci - fied, They laughed and
3. I was so lost____ I should have died, But You have

sent Him from Your side To walk up - on this guilt - y
scorned Him as He died, The hum - ble King they named a
brought me to Your side To be led by Your staff and

sod And to be - come the Lamb of God.____
fraud And sac - ri - ficed the Lamb of God.____
rod, And to be called a lamb of God.____

O_ Lamb of God,____ sweet_ Lamb of God, I love the

ho - ly Lamb of God. O_ wash me in___ His pre-cious_

blood, (1,2) My Je - sus Christ, the Lamb of God.
(3) Till I am just a lamb of God.

His Name Is Life

131

CARMAN LICCIARDELLO
and WILLIAM J. GAITHER

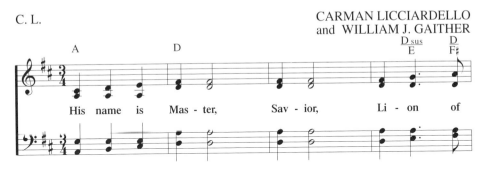

His name is Mas - ter, Sav - ior, Li - on of

Ju - dah, Bless - ed Prince of_ Peace.

O Mighty Cross

I Corinthians 1:18

132

D. B. & J. C.

DAVID BARONI
and JOHN CHISUM

1. O might-y cross, Love lift-ed high, The Lord of life raised there to die; His sac-ri-fice on Cal-va-ry, Has made the might-y cross a tree of life to me.
2. O might-y cross, what throne of grace, He knew no sin, yet took my place; His sac-ri-fice on Cal-va-ry, Has made the might-y cross a tree of life to me.
3. O might-y cross, O Christ so pure, Love held Him there, such shame en-dured; His sac-ri-fice on Cal-va-ry, Has made the might-y cross a tree of life to me.
4. O might-y cross, My soul's re-lease, The stripes He bore, have brought me peace; His sac-ri-fice on Cal-va-ry, Has made the might-y cross a tree of life to me.

133 I Worship You, Almighty God

S. C.-W.

SANDRA CORBETT-WOOD

I wor - ship You, Al - might - y God; there is none like You. I wor - ship You, O Prince of Peace; that is what I want to do. I give You praise, for You are my righ - teous - ness. I

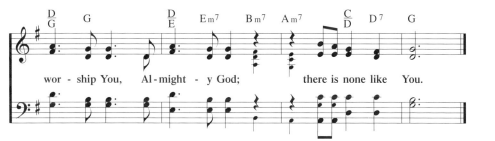

wor - ship You, Al - might - y God; there is none like You.

We Worship and Adore You   134

Psalm 95:6

Unknown   Unknown

We wor - ship and a - dore You, Bow - ing down be -

fore You, Songs of prais - es sing - ing, Hal - le - lu - jahs

ring - ing. Hal - le - lu - jah, hal - le -

lu - jah, hal - le - lu - jah, A - men.

135 Shout to the Lord

D. Z.

DARLENE ZSCHECH

136

Knowing You

Philippians 3:7-11

G. K.

GRAHAM KENDRICK

1. All I once held dear, built my life up - on, all this
2. Now my heart's de - sire is to know You more, To be
3. O to know the pow'r of Your ris - en life and to

137 How Majestic Is Your Name

Psalm 8:1

M. W. S.

MICHAEL W. SMITH

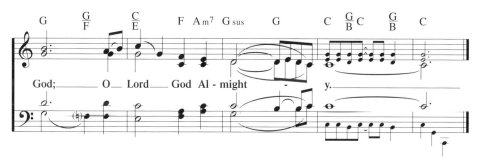

God;___ O_ Lord___ God Al - might - y.___

Let the Redeemed 138
Psalm 107:2

W. E.

WARD ELLIS

Let the re-deemed of the Lord say so, Let the re -

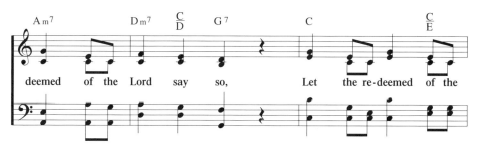

deemed of the Lord say so, Let the re-deemed of the

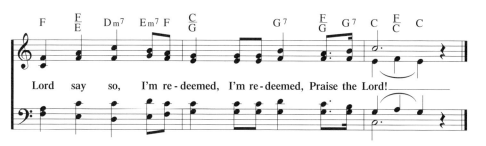

Lord say so, I'm re - deemed, I'm re-deemed, Praise the Lord!___

139 Each Moment with You

M. L. and K. B.

MOSIE LISTER
and KEN BIBLE

1. We treasure these moments, These moments to-
2. We treasure each moment, Each moment to-

gether. With all Your children,
gether. As You go with us

We sing Your praise. For You have
through-out the day. In ev - 'ry

come in love and grace. With joy we worship face to
prob-lem You are there. You fill our lives with praise and

face.
prayer. We trea-sure these mo - ments,

these mo - ments with You.

The Lord Is in This Place   140

Genesis 28:16

M. L.

MOSIE LISTER

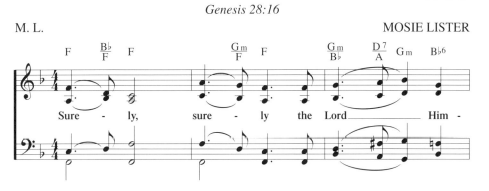

Sure - ly, sure - ly the Lord Him -

self is in this place. Je - sus, Je - sus,

One of Your Children Needs You, Lord

141

M. L.

MOSIE LISTER

1. One of Your chil - dren needs You, Lord.
2. One of Your chil - dren is cry - ing Lord.
3. One of Your chil - dren loves You, Lord.

One of Your chil - dren needs You, Lord.
One of Your chil - dren is cry - ing Lord.
One of Your chil - dren loves You, Lord.

One of Your chil - dren needs You, Lord.
One of Your chil - dren is cry - ing Lord.
One of Your chil - dren loves You, Lord.

Je - sus, Je - sus, be near.

142   We Shall Overcome

Revelation 12:11

J. H.

JACK HAYFORD

Surrendered, Completely Surrendered

143

S. R. A.

STEPHEN R. ADAMS

Sur - ren - dered, com - plete - ly sur - ren - dered;

What - ev - er He wants, I'll o - bey.

Sur - ren - dered, com - plete - ly sur - ren - dered;

His will is my peace for to - day.

144 God Answers Prayer

Psalm 55:17

KEN BIBLE

Traditional

1. God answers prayer in the morn - ing; God an - swers
2. Talk to the Lord in the morn - ing; Talk to the
3. Je - sus is love in the morn - ing; Je - sus is

prayer thro' the day;— God an - swers
Lord thro' the day;— Talk to the
love thro' the day;— Je - sus is

prayer in the ev - 'ning– He hears ev - 'ry
Lord in the ev - 'ning– He's near and He
love in the ev - 'ning– You don't have to

time you pray.
knows your name.

be a -

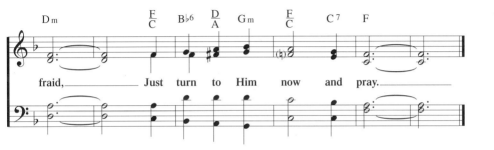

fraid,_____ Just turn to Him now and pray.

The Family of God 145

W. J. and GLORIA GAITHER   WILLIAM J. GAITHER

I'm so glad I'm a part of the fam - 'ly of God—

I've been washed in the foun - tain, cleansed by His blood!

Joint heirs with Je - sus as we trav - el this sod; For I'm

part of the fam - 'ly, the fam - 'ly of God._____

146 Thou Art Worthy

Revelation 4:11; 5:9

P. M. M.

PAULINE M. MILLS

Thou art wor-thy, Thou art wor-thy, Thou art

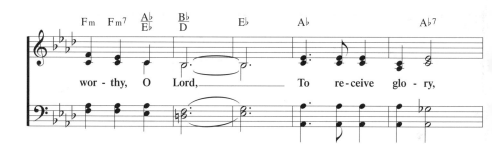

wor-thy, O Lord,_____ To re-ceive glo-ry,

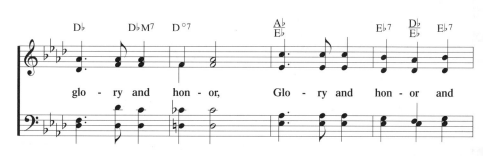

glo-ry and hon-or, Glo-ry and hon-or and

pow'r._____ For Thou hast cre-at-ed, hast

all things cre - at - ed; Thou hast cre - at - ed all

things._____ And for Thy plea - sure they are cre -

at - ed; For Thou art wor - thy, O Lord._____

I Live!

John 14:19

147

R. C.

RICH COOK

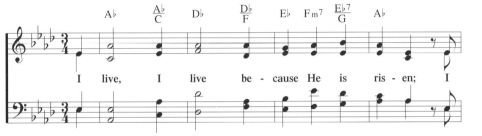

I live, I live be - cause He is ris - en; I

He's All I Need

148

Traditional and KEN BIBLE

Traditional
Arranged by Tom Fettke

1. He's all I need, He's all I
2. He's good to me, He's good to
3. He's life and peace, He's life and

need; Je-sus is all I need.
me; Je-sus is good to me.
peace; Je-sus is life and peace.

He's all I need, He's all I
He's good to me, He's good to
He's life and peace, He's life and

need; Je-sus is all I need.
me; Je-sus is good to me.
peace; Je-sus is life and peace.

149   Shine, Jesus, Shine

G. K.

GRAHAM KENDRICK

150

You Are Holy;
I Come in Silence

Habakkuk 2:20

K. B.

KEN BIBLE

You are ho - ly;___ I come in si - lence.___

___ You are wise,___ Lord;___ I come to hear.___

___ You are God; I come to o - bey.___

You. You are love;___ I come to draw near.___

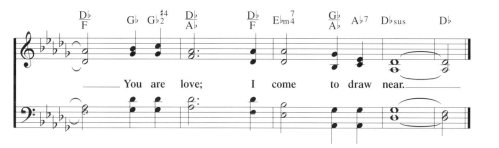

You are love; I come to draw near.

Only Believe

151

Mark 5:36

P. R.

PAUL RADER

On - ly be - lieve, on - ly be - lieve; All things are

pos - si - ble, on - ly be - lieve. On - ly be - lieve,

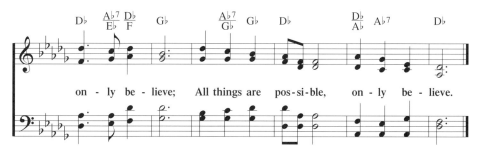

on - ly be - lieve; All things are pos - si - ble, on - ly be - lieve.

152 Where the Spirit of the Lord Is

2 Corinthians 3:17

S. R. A.

STEPHEN R. ADAMS

Where the Spir - it of the Lord is, there is peace;

Where the Spir - it of the Lord is, there is love.

There is com - fort in life's dark - est hour.__ There is

light and life there is help and pow - er In the

Spir - it, in the Spir - it of the Lord.__

Peace in the Midst of the Storm 153

Hebrews 6:19

S. R. A.

STEPHEN R. ADAMS

There is peace in the midst of my storm - tossed life; O there's an
An - chor, there's a Rock to cast my faith up - on—
Je - sus rides in my ves - sel so I'll fear no a -
larm; He gives me peace in the midst of my storm!

154 We Have Come into His House

B. B.

BRUCE BALLINGER

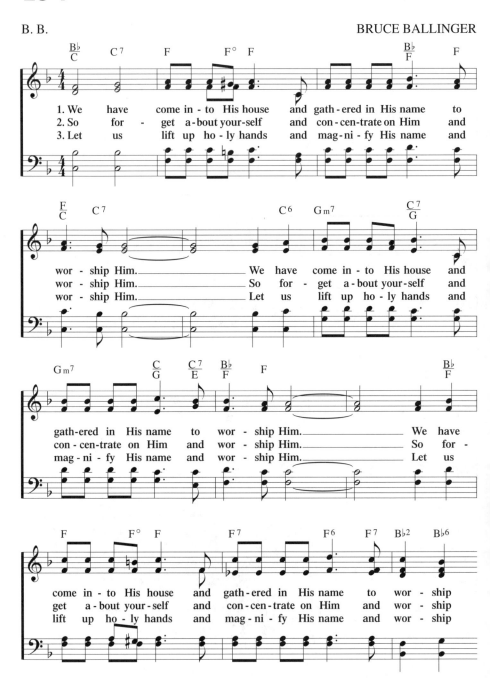

1. We have come in-to His house and gath-ered in His name to
2. So for - get a-bout your-self and con-cen-trate on Him and
3. Let us lift up ho-ly hands and mag-ni-fy His name and

wor - ship Him. We have come in - to His house and
wor - ship Him. So for - get a - bout your-self and
wor - ship Him. Let us lift up ho - ly hands and

gath-ered in His name to wor - ship Him. We have
con - cen-trate on Him and wor - ship Him. So for -
mag - ni - fy His name and wor - ship Him. Let us

come in - to His house and gath-ered in His name to wor - ship
get a - bout your-self and con-cen-trate on Him and wor - ship
lift up ho - ly hands and mag-ni - fy His name and wor - ship

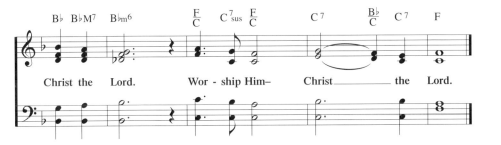

One Flock, One Shepherd 155

John 10:16

S. R. A.

STEPHEN R. ADAMS

156 Philippians 4:13

H. W. G.

HOMER W. GRIMES

When We See Christ

157

2 Corinthians 4:17

E. K. R.

ESTHER KERR RUSTHOI

It will be worth it all____ when we see Je - sus;____

Life's trials will seem so small____ when we see Christ!____

One glimpse of His dear face____ all sor - row will e - rase;____

So brave - ly run the race____ till we see Christ.____

158

All Your Anxiety

I Peter 5:7

E. H. J.

EDWARD HENRY JOY

All your anx - i - e - ty, all your care,

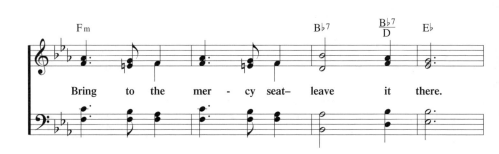

Bring to the mer - cy seat– leave it there.

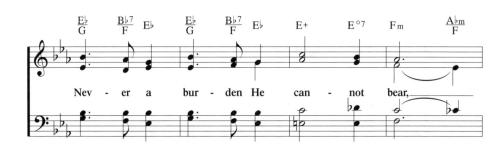

Nev - er a bur - den He can - not bear,

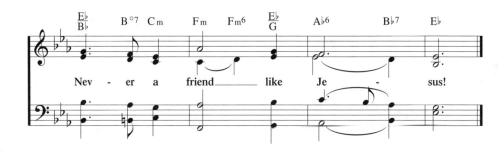

Nev - er a friend like Je - sus!

Seek Ye First

Matthew 6:33

159

K. L.

KAREN LAFFERTY

1. Seek ye first the king - dom of God
2. Ask and it shall be giv - en un - to you;

And His righ - teous - ness;
Seek and you shall find;

And all these things shall be add - ed un - to you.
Knock and it shall be o - pened un - to you.

Hal - le - lu, Hal - le - lu - jah.

160   The Bond of Love

O. S.

OTIS SKILLINGS

Spir - it of God; We are one in the bond of love.

I Love You with the Love of the Lord

161

J. G.

JAMES GILBERT

I__ love you with the love__ of the Lord,

Yes, I love you with the love__ of the Lord.

I can see in you the__ glo - ry of my King,

And I love you with the love__ of the Lord.

162

We Bow Down

T. P.

TWILA PARIS

1. You are Lord of cre - a - tion and Lord of my
2. You are King of cre - a - tion and King of my

life, Lord of the land and the sea.
life, King of the land and the sea.

You were Lord of the heav - en be - fore there was
You were King of the heav - en be - fore there was

time, And Lord of all lords You will be!
time, And King of all kings You will be!

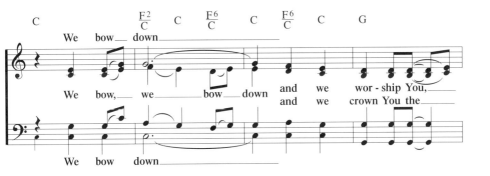

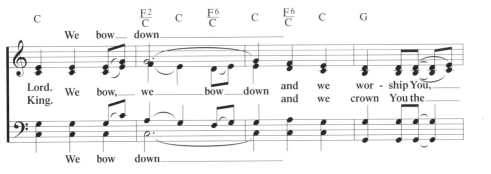

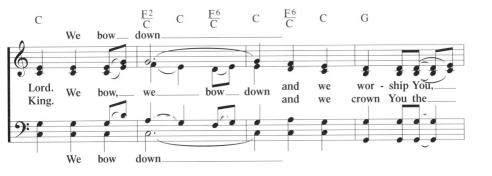

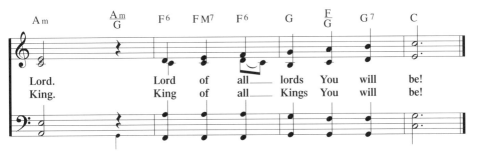

163 Saved to Tell Others

Hollywood Gospel Team

ARTHUR WOOLSEY

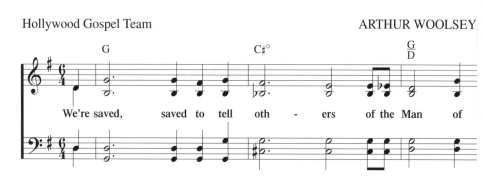

We're saved, saved to tell oth - ers of the Man of

Gal - i - lee. Saved, saved to live dai - ly for the

Christ of Cal - va - ry. Saved, saved to in - vite

you to His sal - va - tion free. We're saved, saved,

saved by His blood for all e - ter - ni - ty.

Thank You, Lord 164

B. S. and S. S.

BESSIE and SETH SYKES

Thank You, Lord, for sav - ing my soul; Thank You, Lord, for

mak - ing me whole; Thank You, Lord, for giv - ing to

me Thy great sal - va - tion so rich and free.

165 When I Look Into Your Holiness

W. P. and C. P.

WAYNE and CATHY PERRIN

When I look in-to Your ho - li - ness,_____ When I gaze in-to Your love - li - ness, When all things that sur-round be-come shad-ows in the light of You,_____ When I've found the joy of reach-ing Your heart,_____ When my

166 Great and Wonderful

Revelation 15:3-4

Adapted by S. D.

STUART DAUERMANN

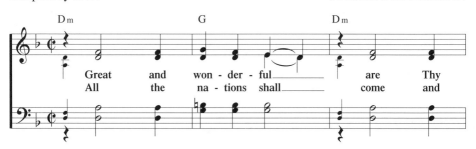

Great and won - der - ful _____ are Thy
All the na - tions shall_____ come and

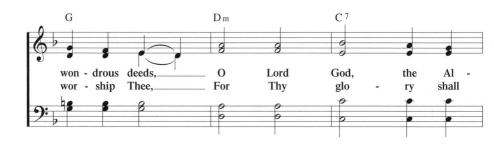

won - drous deeds,_____ O Lord God, the Al -
wor - ship Thee,_____ For Thy glo - ry shall

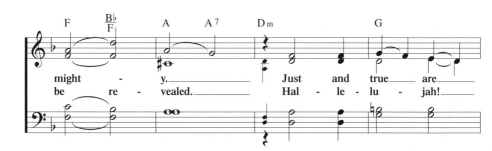

might - y._____ Just and true___ are___
be re - vealed._____ Hal - le - lu - jah!_____

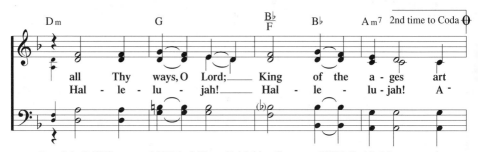

all Thy ways, O Lord;___ King of the a - ges art
Hal - le - lu - jah!_____ Hal - le - lu - jah! A -

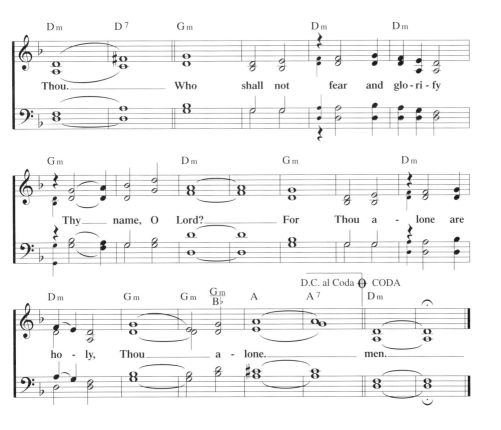

Thou._____ Who shall not fear and glo-ri-fy Thy_____ name, O Lord?_____ For Thou a - lone are ho - ly, Thou_____ a - lone._____ men.

D.C. al Coda CODA

I'm Forever Grateful 167

M. A.
MARK ALTROGGE

You did not wait for me_____ to draw near to You,_____ But You clothed Your-self with frail hu-man-i - ty; You

Love Through Me

168

M. L.

MOSIE LISTER

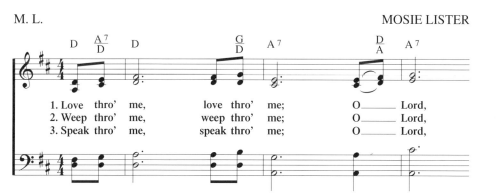

1. Love thro' me, love thro' me; O_____ Lord,
2. Weep thro' me, weep thro' me; O_____ Lord,
3. Speak thro' me, speak thro' me; O_____ Lord,

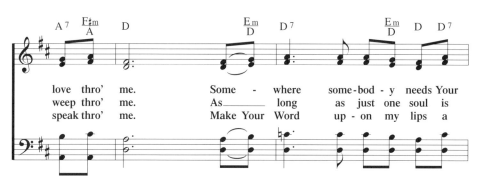

love thro' me. Some - where some-bod - y needs Your
weep thro' me. As_____ long as just one soul is
speak thro' me. Make Your Word up - on my lips a

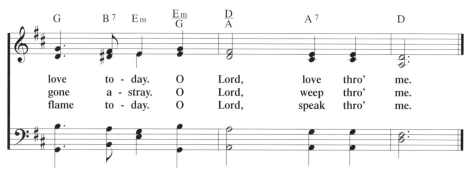

love to - day. O Lord, love thro' me.
gone a - stray. O Lord, weep thro' me.
flame to - day. O Lord, speak thro' me.

169 The Trees of the Field

Isaiah 55:12

Adapted by
STEFFI GEISER RUBIN

STUART DAUERMANN

You shall go out with joy and be led forth with peace.

The moun-tains and the hills will break forth be-

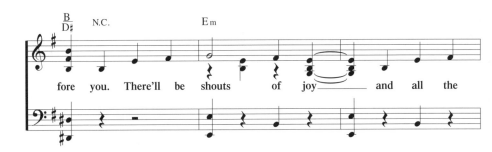

fore you. There'll be shouts of joy and all the

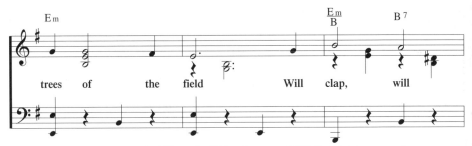

trees of the field Will clap, will

170 I Will Serve Thee

I John 4:19

W. J. and GLORIA GAITHER

WILLIAM J. GAITHER

I will serve Thee be-cause I love Thee;
I was noth - ing be - fore You found me;

You have giv - en life to me.
You have giv - en

life to me. Heart - aches, bro - ken

piec - es, Ru - ined lives are why You died on

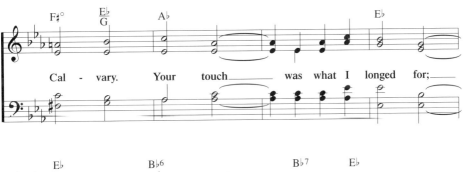

Cal - vary. Your touch_____ was what I longed for;_____

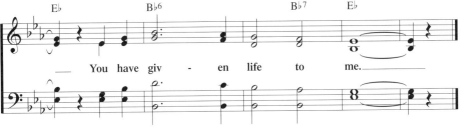

_____ You have giv - en life to me._____

Be Bold, Be Strong

171

Haggai 2:4; I Corinthians 16:13

M. C.

MORRIS CHAPMAN

Be bold! (be bold!) Be strong! (be strong!) For the

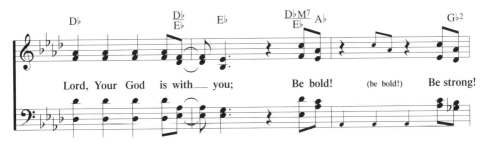

Lord, Your God is with___ you; Be bold! (be bold!) Be strong!

Song for the Nations

172

Matthew 28:19

C. C.

CHRIS CHRISTENSEN

1. May we be a shin - ing light to the na - tions, A shin - ing
2. May we bring a word of hope to the na - tions, A word of
3. May we be a heal - ing balm to the na - tions, A heal - ing
4. May we sing a song of joy to the na - tions, A song of
5. May Your king - dom come to the na - tions, Your will be

light to the peo - ples of the earth, Till the whole world sees the
life to the peo - ples of the earth, Till the whole world knows there's sal -
balm to the peo - ples of the earth, Till the whole world knows the
praise to the peo - ples of the earth, Till the whole world rings with the
done to the peo - ples of the earth, Till the whole world knows that

glo - ry of Your name. May Your pure light shine thro' us.
va - tion thro' Your name. May Your mer - cy flow thro' us.
pow - er of Your name. May Your heal - ing flow thro' us.
prais - es of Your name. May Your song be sung thro' us.
Je - sus Christ is Lord. May Your king - dom come in us.

173   I Will Lift High

Scripture Reference

D. W.

DAN WHITTEMORE

I will lift high___ the Lord God at all times. I will sing His praise the rest of my years. I sought the Lord___ and He gra-cious-ly an-swered. He took away___ from me my great-est fear. He took away___ from me my great-est fear.___ For the

He took a-way___ from me my great - est fear.

He took a-way___ from me my great - est fear.___

174 Ah, Lord God

Jeremiah 32:17

K. C.

KAY CHANCE

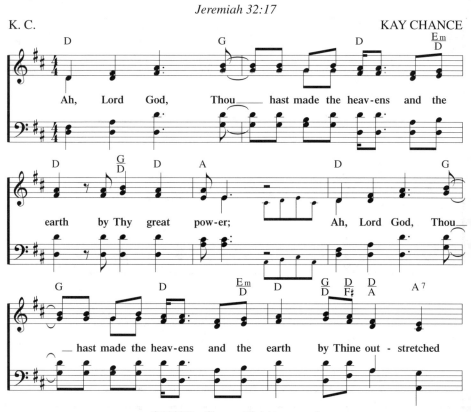

Ah, Lord God, Thou___ hast made the heav-ens and the

earth by Thy great pow-er; Ah, Lord God, Thou___

___ hast made the heav-ens and the earth by Thine out - stretched

175   Great and Mighty

M. B.

MARLENE BIGLEY

Lord our God,_____ Great and might - y is He.

I'm So Glad Jesus Lifted Me 176

Psalm 40:1-3

Traditional and
CAMP KIRKLAND

Traditional

1. I'm___ so___ glad Je - sus lift - ed me, I'm___ so___ glad,
2. I was lost in sin, Je - sus res-cued me, I was lost in sin,
3. Now I'm heav-en-bound, Je - sus set me free, Now I'm heav-en-bound,

Je - sus lift - ed me: I'm___ so___ glad, Je - sus lift - ed me
Je - sus res-cued me; I was lost in sin, Je - sus res-cued me,
Je - sus set me free; Now I'm heav-en-bound, Je - sus set me free,

Sing - ing, "Glo - ry, hal - le - lu - jah!" Je - sus lift - ed me.
Sing - ing, "Glo - ry, hal - le - lu - jah!" Je - sus lift - ed me.
Sing - ing, "Glo - ry, hal - le - lu - jah!" Je - sus lift - ed me.

177 They'll Know We Are Christians by Our Love

John 13:35

P. S.

PETER SCHOLTES

1. We are one in the Spir-it, we are one in the Lord,
2. We will walk with each oth-er, we will walk hand in hand,
3. We will work with each oth-er, we will work side by side,
4. All___ praise to the Fa-ther, from___ whom all things come,

We are one in the Spir-it, we are one in the Lord,
We will walk with each oth-er, we will walk hand in hand,
We will work with each oth-er, we will work side by side,
And all praise to Christ Je-sus, His___ on - ly___ Son,

And we pray that all u - ni-ty may one day be re - stored:
And to-geth - er we'll spread the news that God is in our land:
And we'll guard each one's dig-ni-ty and save___ each one's pride:
And all praise to the Spir-it, who___ makes___ us___ one:

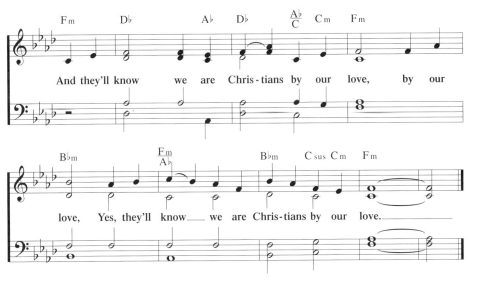

And they'll know we are Chris-tians by our love, by our love, Yes, they'll know___ we are Chris-tians by our love.___

Great Is the Lord 178

Psalm 145:3

M.W.S. & D.D.S.

MICHAEL W. SMITH
and DEBORAH D. SMITH

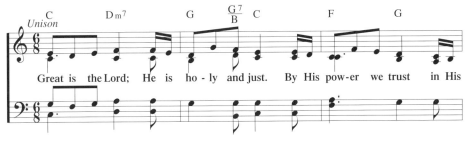

Great is the Lord; He is ho - ly and just. By His pow-er we trust in His

love.___ Great is the Lord; He is faith-ful and true. By His

My Tribute

Psalm 116:12

179

A. C.

ANDRAE CROUCH

Lyrics:
How can I say thanks for the things You have done for me— Things so un-de-served, yet You give to prove Your love for me? The voic-es of a mil-lion an-gels could not ex-press my grat-i-tude. All that I

180

Holy, Holy, Holy
Is the Lord of Hosts

Isaiah 6:3

Adapted by N. P.

NOLENE PRINCE

whole earth is full of His glo - ry,_____ Ho - ly is_____ the Lord.

O Lord, How Wonderful You Are   **181**

Psalm 8:1

M. L.   MOSIE LISTER

O Lord, how won - der - ful You are,_____ How high and

ho - ly in the heav - ens! You bro't us high - er, high - er than the

high - est star. O Lord, how won - der - ful You are!

182 Everything Within Me Worships You

S. S.

SUSAN SACCA

You. Ev-'ry-thing with-in me wor-ships You.

Faith in God Can Move a Mountain

183

Matthew 17:20

J. W. P., A. E. S.
and G.M.W.-B.

JOHN W. PETERSON,
ALFRED E. SMITH and
GRACE MARILYN WATKINS-BOLTON

Faith in God can move a might-y moun-tain,
Faith can calm the trou-bled sea, Faith can make the des-ert like a
foun-tain, Faith can bring the vic-to-ry

184 Crown Him King of Kings

S. D.

SHARON DAMAZIO

He shall reign, He shall reign for - ev - er - more.

What a Mighty God We Serve 185

Unknown

Unknown
Arranged by Keith Phillips

What a might - y God we serve.

What a might - y God we serve.

An - gels bow be - fore Him, heav'n and earth a -

dore Him; What a might - y God we serve.

186 Open Our Eyes

B. C.

BOB CULL

O - pen our eyes, Lord,_____ we want to see
O - pen our ears, Lord,_____ and help us to

Je - sus;_____ To reach out and touch
lis - ten._____ O - pen our eyes,

Him_____ and say that we love Him._____

Lord,_____ we want to see Je - sus._____

This Is My Prayer 187

D. H.

DOUG HOLCK

188 Only You

KEN BIBLE

STEVEN V. TAYLOR

All my hope, all my joy– on - ly You.

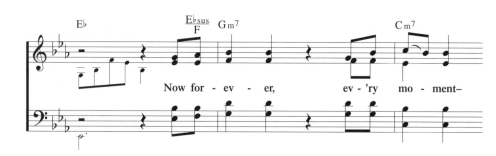

Now for - ev - er, ev - 'ry mo - ment–

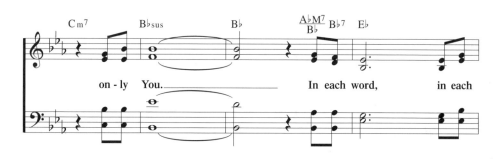

on - ly You. In each word, in each

deed, not my - self, not my strength, On - ly

You, Liv-ing Christ, on-ly You.

Christ in Us Be Glorified 189

Philippians 1:20

M. C.

MORRIS CHAPMAN

Christ in us be glo-ri-fied, Christ in us be lift - ed high; Let His love be shown and His prais-es be known, Let Christ be glo - ri - fied, Let Christ be glo - ri - fied.

190 Lifting Up My Voice

D. W.

DAN WHITTEMORE

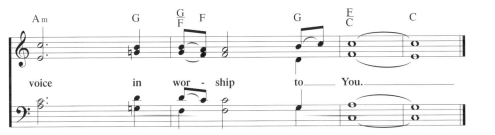

My Desire 191

L. P.

LILLIAN PLANKENHORN

192 Jesus, Draw Me Close

R. F.

RICK FOUNDS

Je - sus, draw___ me close,_____ clos - er, Lord,___ to You.__

Let the world___ a-round___ me fade a-way.__

Je - sus, draw___ me close,__

clos - er, Lord,___ to You,___ For

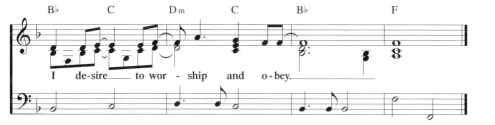

I de-sire to wor-ship and o-bey.

I Love You, Lord 193

L. K.

LAURIE KLEIN

I love You, Lord, and I lift my voice To

wor - ship You; O my soul, re - joice! Take

joy, my King, in what You hear;

May it be a sweet, sweet sound in Your ear.

194 He Is Our Peace

Ephesians 2:14; 1 Peter 5:7

Adapted by K. G.

KANDELA GROVES

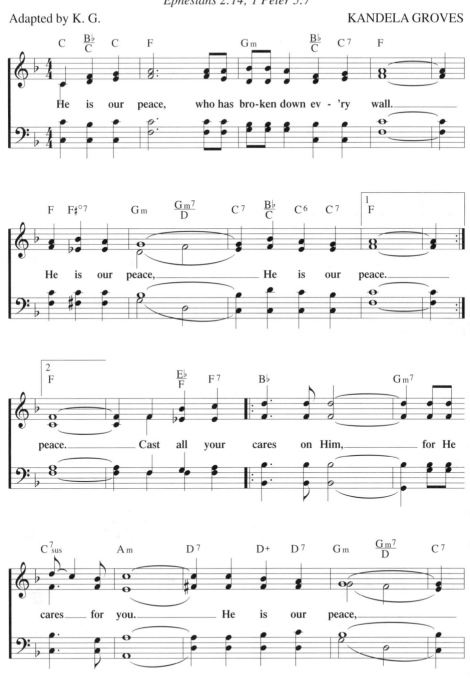

He is our peace, who has bro-ken down ev - 'ry wall.

He is our peace, He is our peace.

peace. Cast all your cares on Him, for He

cares for you. He is our peace,

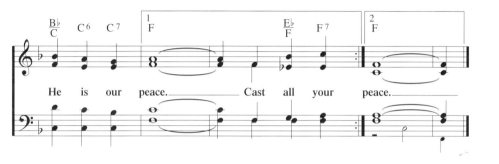

He is our peace. Cast all your peace.

He Is Lord 195

Philippians 2:11

Adapted   Unknown

He is Lord, He is Lord! He is ris-en from the

dead and He is Lord! Ev-'ry knee shall bow, ev-'ry

tongue con - fess That Je - sus Christ is Lord.

196 Step by Step

Psalm 63:1

D. S.

DAVID STRASSER

O God, You are my God, and I will ev-er praise You. O God, You are my God, and I will ev-er praise You. I will seek You in the morn - ing and I will learn to walk in Your way; And step by step You'll lead

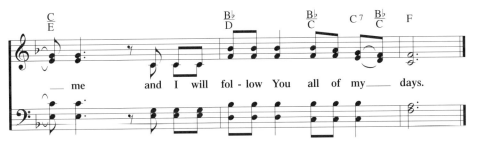

me and I will fol-low You all of my days.

Alleluia

197

JERRY SINCLAIR

J. S.

1. Al - le - lu - ia, al - le - lu - ia, Al - le -
2. He's my Sav - ior; He's my Sav - ior. He's my
3. He is wor - thy; He is wor - thy. He is
4. I will praise Him; I will praise Him. I will

lu - ia, al - le - lu - ia, Al - le - lu - ia, al - le -
Sav - ior; He's my Sav - ior. He's my Sav - ior; He's my
wor - thy; He is wor - thy. He is wor - thy; He is
praise Him; I will praise Him. I will praise Him; I will

lu - ia, Al - le - lu - ia, al - le - lu - ia!
Sav - ior. He's my Sav - ior; He's my Sav - ior.
wor - thy. He is wor - thy; He is wor - thy.
praise Him. I will praise Him; I will praise Him.

198 You Are the Light

Psalm 36:9; John 14:6

KEN BIBLE

TOM FETTKE

1. You are the Light– we see. You are the Truth– we know. You are the Life– we live. You are the Hope, You are the Joy, You are the Song we sing.

2. With-in our hearts– Your light. With-in our minds– Your truth. With-in our lives– Your love. Liv-ing Your hope, Sing-ing Your beau-ti-ful song.

I've Got Peace like a River 199

Isaiah 48:18

Spiritual
Arranged by Lyndell Leatherman

1. I've got peace like a riv-er, I've got peace like a riv-er, I've got peace like a riv-er in my soul.
2. I've got love like an o-cean, I've got love like an o-cean, I've got love like an o-cean in my soul.
3. I've got joy like a foun-tain, I've got joy like a foun-tain, I've got joy like a foun-tain in my soul.

200 Wonderful

H. L.

HALDOR LILLENAS

Won - der - ful, won - der - ful, Je - sus is to me!

Coun - sel - or, Prince of Peace, Might - y God is He!

Sav - ing me, keep - ing me from all sin and shame,

Won - der - ful is my Re - deem - er; praise His name!

Your Love Compels Me

201

2 Corinthians 5:14

D. H.

DOUG HOLCK

202 Come into His Presence

Psalm 100:4

L. B.

LYNN BAIRD

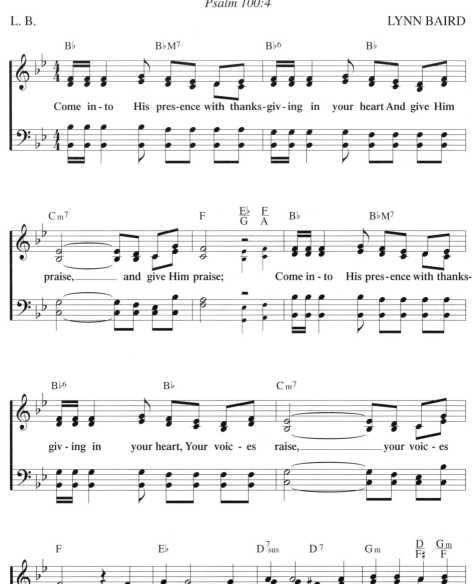

Come in-to His pres-ence with thanks-giv-ing in your heart And give Him praise,_____ and give Him praise; Come in-to His pres-ence with thanks-giv-ing in your heart, Your voic-es raise,_____ your voic-es raise. Give glo-ry and hon-or_____ and pow-er un-to

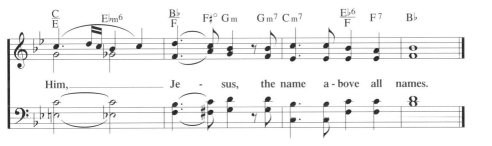

Him,_____ Je - sus, the name a - bove all names.

He Is Here

203

K. T.

KIRK TALLEY

He is here, hal - le - lu - jah! He is here, a - men!

He is here, ho - ly, ho - ly, I will bless His name a - gain.___

He is here; lis - ten close - ly. Hear Him call - ing out___ your name.

He is here; you can touch Him. You will nev - er be___ the same.

204 When the Battle's Over

2 Timothy 4:8

HARRIETTE WATERS

A. E. LIND

And when the bat - tle's o - ver, we shall wear a crown! Yes,

we shall wear a crown! Yes, we shall wear a crown! And

when the bat - tle's o - ver, we shall wear a crown in the

new Je - ru - sa - lem. Wear a crown, wear a crown,
Wear a crown, wear a crown,

Wear a bright and shin - ing crown. And when the bat-tle's o - ver,

we shall wear a crown in the new Je - ru - sa - lem.

Got Any Rivers? 205

O. C. E.

OSCAR C. ELIASON

Got an - y riv - ers you think are un - cross - a - ble? Got an - y

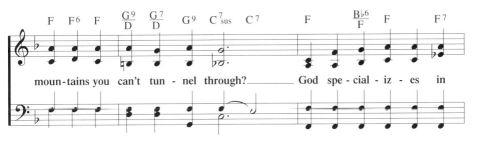

moun - tains you can't tun - nel through?_____ God spe - cial - iz - es in

things thought im - pos - si - ble– He does the things oth - ers can - not do.

206

What the Lord
Has Done in Me

R. M.

REUBEN MORGAN

Let the weak say I am strong. Let the poor say I am rich. _____ Let the blind say I can see. _____ It's what the Lord has done in me. Let the me. Ho - san - na, ho - san - na to the Lamb that was slain. Ho -

san - na, ho - san - na, Je-sus died and rose a-gain.

God Is Good All the Time 207

Psalm 136:1

D. M. and P. O.

DON MOEN and
PAUL OVERSTREET

God is good all the time; He put a song of praise____ in this

heart of mine. God is good all the time; thro' the dark - est night____ His

light will shine. God is good, God is good all the time.____

208 I Humble Myself Before You

B. W.

BRUCE WICKERSHEIM

Ho - ly One; You are the Righ-teous Judge, Cre - a - tor of all life, and Sus - tain - er of my soul._____ I hum-ble-ness, Lord, I mag - ni - fy Your name.

2 Corinthians 3:18 209

Adapted

Unknown

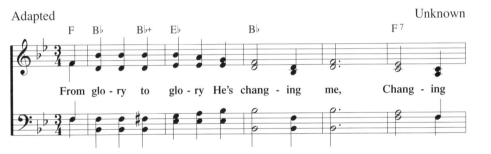

From glo - ry to glo - ry He's chang - ing me, Chang - ing

Behold

Isaiah 12:2

210

S. D.

STUART DAUERMANN

211

Declare His Glory

M. L.

MOSIE LISTER

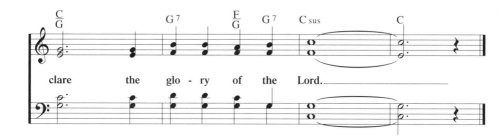

clare the glo - ry of the Lord.

212 Broken for You
I Corinthians 11:23-26

J. H.

JACK HAYFORD

This is my bod - y that is bro - ken for you.

This is the cov - e - nant that Christ now re - news.

My life for yours,____ that your life may be Mine; This

213

Yes, Lord, Yes

L. K.

LYNN KEESECKER

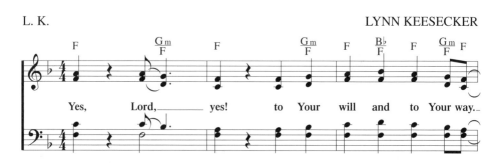

Yes, Lord,____ yes! to Your will and to Your way.

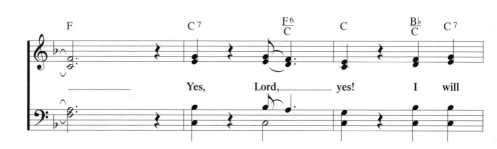

____ Yes, Lord,____ yes! I will

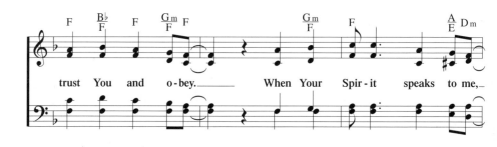

trust You and o - bey.____ When Your Spir - it speaks to me,

____ with my whole heart I'll a - gree____ And my

We'll Work Till Jesus Comes 214

ELIZABETH MILLS   WILLIAM MILLER

215   O How He Loves You and Me

John 15:13

K. K.

KURT KAISER

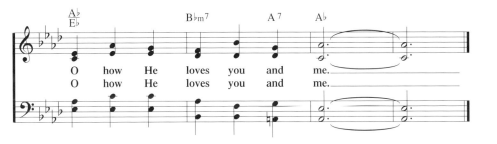

O   how   He   loves   you   and   me.
O   how   He   loves   you   and   me.

Jesus Is the Sweetest Name I Know   216

L. L.

LELA LONG

Je - sus is the sweet-est name I   know,   And He's just   the same

as   His   love - ly name,   And   that's the rea - son why I   love Him

so.   O   Je - sus   is   the sweet - est name I   know!

217 There Is a Redeemer

M. G.

MELODY GREEN

1. There is a Re - deem - er, Je - sus, God's own Son;
2. Je - sus, my Re - deem - er, name a - bove all names;
3. When I stand in Glo - ry, I will see His face;

Pre - cious Lamb of God, Mes - si - ah, Ho - ly One.
Pre - cious Lamb of God, Mes - si - ah, O for sin - ners slain.
There I'll serve my King for - ev - er In that ho - ly place.

Thank You, oh, my Fa - ther, for giv - ing us Your Son, And

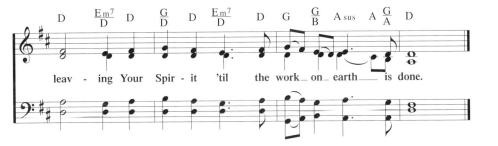

leav - ing Your Spir - it 'til the work_ on_ earth___ is done.

I Love Him Better Every Day 218

THORO HARRIS

SIDNEY E. COX

I love Him bet-ter ev-'ry day, ev-'ry day. I love Him

bet-ter ev-'ry day, ev-'ry day. Close by His side

I will a-bide. I love Him bet-ter ev-'ry day.

219 No Other Name

Acts 4:12; Philippians 2:9-11

R. G.

ROBERT GAY

No oth-er name but the name___ of Je-sus, No oth-er

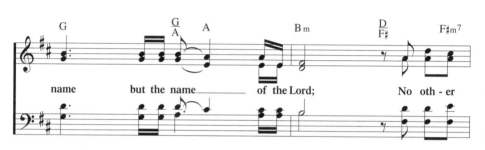

name but the name___ of the Lord; No oth-er

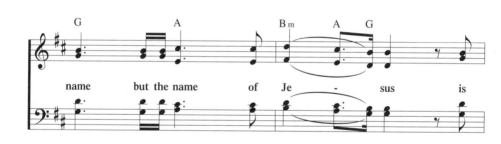

name but the name of Je - sus is

wor - thy of glo-ry, and wor - thy of hon-or, And

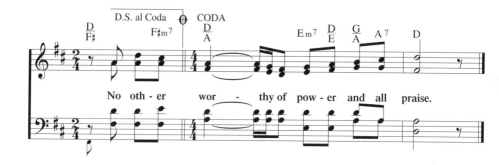

No oth - er wor - thy of pow - er and all praise.

220

Spirit Song

J. W.

JOHN WIMBER

1. O let the Son of God en - fold you with His
2. O come and sing the song with glad - ness as your

Spir - it and His love; Let Him fill your heart and
hearts are filled with joy; Lift your hands in sweet sur -

sat - is - fy your soul. O let Him
ren - der to His name. O give Him

This index is provided for the use of worship leaders who want to plan their own worship sequences or medleys. By referring to the keys and meter signatures, such medleys can be planned with the proper balance of continuity and variety.

Surely the Presence of the Lord Is in This Place (D) 104
The Lord Is in This Place (F). 140
Where the Spirit of the Lord Is (E♭) 152

Heaven *(See "Eternal Life & The Second Coming")*

Holiness

Change My Heart, O God (D) 64
Christ in Us Be Glorified (E♭) 189
2 Corinthians 3:18 (B♭) 209
Every Moment of Every Day (B♭). 37
Everything Within Me Worships You (F) 182
I Live! (A♭). 147
I Live by Faith (F) 98
Knowing You (C) 136
Let the Beauty of Jesus Be Seen in Me (D♭) . . . 54
More of You (B♭) 26
My Life Is in You, Lord (G) 111
Only You (E♭) 188
Sanctuary (E♭) 65
Shine, Jesus, Shine (A♭) 149
Spirit of the Living God (F) 40
Surrendered, Completely Surrendered (C). . . . 143
Take My Life (F) 12

Holy Spirit

Come, Holy Spirit (F) 42
Come Just As You Are (F) 66
Dare to Run (G) 125
Father, I Adore You (F) 53
Holy Spirit, Thou Art Welcome (B♭) 36
Let the Beauty of Jesus Be Seen in Me (D♭) . . . 54
Let There Be an Anointing (F) 82
My Desire (C) 191
Sanctuary (E♭) 65
Spirit of the Living God (F) 40
Spirit Song (D). 220
The Bond of Love (A♭) 160
There Is a Redeemer (D) 217
They'll Know We Are Christians by Our Love (F min) 177
Where the Spirit of the Lord Is (E♭) 152
Yes, Lord, Yes (F) 213

Invitation

Come Just As You Are (F) 66
I Come to the Cross (F) 24
I Have Decided to Follow Jesus (C) 70
Into My Heart (F) 67
Let Go and Let God Have His Way (F) 127

Jesus Christ – Lordship

Above All (A♭) 122
All Hail King Jesus (F) 2
Crown Him King of Kings (A♭) 184
He Is Lord (F) 195
His Name Is Life (D). 131
His Name Is Wonderful (F) 8
Hosanna (G). 117
Jesus Is Lord (C) 97

Jesus Is Lord of All (F) . . . . 8〔
No Other Name (D) . . . . 21〔
Our God Reigns (B♭) . . . . 9〔
Shine, Jesus, Shine (A♭) . . . . 14〔
Shout to the North (F). . . . . 4〔
Sovereign Lord (A♭) . . . . 3〔
We Bow Down (C). . . . . 16〔
Worthy, You Are Worthy (E♭) . . . . 5〔

Jesus Christ – Resurrection

I Live! (A♭). . . . . 14〔
Jesus Is Lord (C). . . . . 9〔
Knowing You (C) . . . . 13〔
Our God Reigns (B♭). . . . . 9〔

Jesus Christ – Suffering, Death, & Atonement

Above All (A♭) . . . . 12〔
For God So Loved the World (F) . . . . 7〔
Grace Alone (C) . . . . 9〔
Hallelujah! Praise the Lamb (F) . . . . 3〔
He Is Our Peace (F) 194
I Come to the Cross (F) . . . . 2〔
I Live by Faith (F) . . . . 9〔
I Love Him (C). . . . . 〔
I Will Serve Thee (E♭) . . . . 17〔
I'm Forever Grateful (A) 167
Lamb of God (C). . . . . 13〔
Lift Up the Cross (A♭) . . . . 10〔
O How He Loves You and Me (A♭). 215
O Mighty Cross (D) . . . . 13〔
Our God Reigns (B♭). . . . . 9〔
Saved to Tell Others (G) . . . . 16〔
There Is a Redeemer (D). 217
We Shall Overcome (C) 142
What the Lord Has Done in Me (C) 206
Worthy, You Are Worthy (E♭) . . . . 5〔
Your Are My All in All (F) 94

Majesty of God

Almighty (E♭) . . . . 2〔
Arise, Shine (C) . . . . 34〔
Awesome God (E min). 1
Be Exalted, O God (B♭) . . . . 56〔
Blessed Be the Lord God Almighty (B♭) . . . . . 1〔
Crown Him King of Kings (A♭) . . . . 184〔
Declare His Glory (C) 211
Glorify Thy Name (B♭). . . . . 3〔
Great and Wonderful (D min) 166
Great Is the Lord (C). . . . . 178〔
How Majestic Is Your Name (C) 137
I Exalt Thee (F) . . . . 15〔
I Humble Myself Before You (G min) . . . . . . 208〔
I Stand in Awe (A) 121
Majesty (B♭) . . . . 74〔
Shine, Jesus, Shine (A♭) . . . . 149〔
Shout to the Lord (B♭) 135
Sovereign Lord (A♭) . . . . 30〔
To Him Who Sits on the Throne (C). . . . . . . 89〔
We Will Glorify (D) . . . . 23〔